ACCORDING
— to —
MATTHEW

Clare Richards

Blackie

Blackie & Son Ltd
Bishopbriggs, Glasgow G64 2NZ
7 Leicester Place, London WC2H 7BP

British Library Cataloguing in Publication Data

Richards, Clare
    According to Matthew.
    1. Bible. N.T. Matthew——Critical studies
    I. Title
    226'.206

    ISBN 0-216-92619-X   Schools ed.
    ISBN 0-216-92620-3

Printed in Great Britain by Bell and Bain Ltd., Glasgow

Preface

This book completes a trilogy. I have already tried to look at Jesus through the eyes of Mark and Luke. It would seem that these books, *According to Mark* and *According to Luke* have prompted teachers, particularly in Northern Ireland, to ask for a third, *According to Matthew*.

I hope this new book will not only be useful for those studying the Gospel at GCSE level, but also for people engaged in biblical studies at all levels. The three books could be used by anyone wishing to make a full study of the Synoptic Gospels.

This book focuses on Jesus as seen through Matthew's eyes. I have arranged my material with the GCSE examination syllabus very much in mind. After a general introduction to 'Gospel' the book is divided into four parts:

> The Law
> The Prophets
> The Promised Deliverer
> The Community.

Within the framework of these themes, I have looked at Jesus' life and teaching, as illustrated in texts from the Old and the New Testament.

I have made the link with today's world by using contemporary photographs and encouraging the students to look at 20th century issues and personalities. Each topic concludes with questions, discussion points and ideas to help students to know, understand and evaluate the material.

Since most schools use the text of the *Good News Bible*, I have taken all quotations from that version (unless otherwise indicated). But whether students use this version or another, it is essential that they know the Gospel text.

A Gospel is not a simple biography of Jesus. It is a sophisticated theological document. For this reason I have tried to include difficult and critical arguments. Any over-simplification would distort the truth.

I have tried to present the Gospel in an objective, impartial way, stating both traditional views and the more liberal views of recent scholars. I recognize that teachers in denominational schools will want to supplement the material. I hope I have given them the framework within which they can examine their own traditions.

Acknowledgements

This book is for Doris Hipper who really understands Matthew's Gospel because she always puts people first.
The author and publishers are grateful to the following for permission to reproduce copyright material.

Text
All the quotations from the Old and New Testaments are from the *Good News Bible*, © American Bible Society, 1966, 1971, 1976 published by The Bible Societies and Collins.
Faber and Faber Ltd for the extract from *The Last Temptation* by Nikos Kazantzakis on page 1 and *Journey of the Magi* by T S Eliot on page 78
The Reform Synagogues of Great Britain for the extract from *Forms of Prayer for Jewish Worship* 1977 on page 8
Peter de Rosa for *Jesus the Jew* on page 11
Andre Deutsch Ltd for the extract from *Son of Man* by Dennis Potter, 1979 on page 13
The Universe for the extract on page 18
Catholic Worker Farm, Virginia for the extract from *Easy Essays* by Peter Maurin on page 33
McCrimmon's for the extracts from *The Sacraments for Children* by Hubert Richards, 1988 on page 43 and *Tomorrow's Parish* by Adrian Smith, 1983, on page 117
The Observer for the extract on page 54
Water Authorities Association for the advert on page 68
Stainer and Bell Ltd for *If you are a son of man* by Sydney Carter on page 86 and *Said Judas to Mary . . .* by Sydney Carter on page 89
The Iona Community, Glasgow for the extract from *One Way Left* by George F McLeod on page 87
Ben Henze for *New Testament Answer* on page 99
Oxfam for *Streetwise in Brazil* on page 99
Kevin Hayhew for the poem 'Resurrection' from *Prayers for Peacemakers* 1988 by Sadako Kurihara on page 100
Chatto and Windus for the extract from *Spots of Time* by Basil Willey on page 105
Churchman Publishing Ltd for the extract from *The Trial of Faith* by Archbishop Desmond Tutu on page 106
CUP for the extract from *Christ, Faith and History* by Don Cupitt, 1972 on page 115
The Tablet for the extract on page 119
Owl's Head Press for the poem 'The Lesson' from *Birds of Fire* by Don Linehan, 1985 on page 120

Photographs
The Art Institute of Chicago cover
Sonia Halliday Photographs page 1
John Fisher pages 2, 39, 43 top, 53 left, 62, 74, 81, 82, 87, 105
Clive Lawton, Board of Deputies of British Jews pages 8, 9
Barnaby's Picture Library pages 11, 17, 47 centre, 49, 53 right, 60, 100, 115 top, 116

UNRWA pages 12 (photographer George Nehmeh), 18, 28 (photographer Z Haider), 31 (photographer Munir Nasr), 34, 45 (photographer Munir Nasr), 56, 67 bottom right (photographer George Nehmeh), 72 (photographer Jack Madvo), 79, 80 (photographer Odd Uhrbom), 89 (photographer Kay Brennan), 90 (photographer Munir Nasr), 91 left (photographer George Nehmeh), 101 (photographer Munir Nasr)
Jack Moore pages 13, 113
Carlos Reyes, Andes Press Agency pages 15, 27, 44, 117
Paternoster Church, Mount of Olives page 19
Eastern Daily Press pages 21, 47 top
Medical Missionaries of Mary pages 24, 26 left
Richard Harman page 26 right
Palm Tree Press page 32
Associated Press page 35
Duncan Paul Associates page 36
Anthony Pearce page 40
Rt Rev Dr J Mehaffey pages 43 bottom, 91
BIPAC page 51
Frank Spooner Pictures page 54
Controller of Her Majesty's Stationery Office page 61
Mary Anne Felton page 63
London-Irish News page 67 top
Ingrid Bernard page 67 bottom left
Water Authorities Association page 68
Museo Sacro—Saneto Sanetorum, Rome page 69
The Mansell Collection page 85
Commissioners of Public Works, Ireland page 88
The Council of Christians and Jews page 92
The British Museum page 94
The Independent page 96
Syndication International page 99
Norwich Cathedral page 103
Diocese of East Anglia page 107
The Glasgow Herald page 111
Mike Fisher page 115 bottom
Fr Dennis Finbow page 119

Any photograph not acknowledged above was supplied by the author.

Illustrations
Lucy Clibban pages 5, 6
Norwich Third World Centre page 23
Mark Bennett pages 48, 90, 117
Debra Mallett pages 64, 65
Blanca Richards page 70
Michael Parfitt page 75
Rebecca O'Shea page 78
Sarah Crowe page 106

All remaining illustrations by the author.

Contents

Part A

Part B

Part C

Part D

Introduction to Matthew's Gospel

A few years ago a Greek novelist, Nikos Kazantzakis, wrote a book called *The Last Temptation*. In it he described how Matthew, the tax-collector, although despised by most people, was chosen by Jesus to be one of the apostles. Kazantzakis then wrote this:

> *When the meal ended and all the others lay down to sleep, Matthew knelt below the lamp, drew out the virgin notebook from his shirt, took his quill from behind his ear, leaned over the blank pages and remained meditating for a long time. How should he begin? God had placed him next to this holy man (Jesus) in order that he might faithfully record the words he said and the miracles he performed, so that they would not perish and that future generations might learn about them and choose, in their turn, the road to salvation. Surely that was the duty God had entrusted to him. He knew how to read and write; therefore he had a heavy responsibility: to catch with his pen all that was about to perish and by placing it on paper, to make it immortal. Let the disciples distrust him, let them not want to frequent his presence because once he was a publican. He would show them that the repentant sinner is better than the man who has never sinned.*
>
> *He plunged his quill into the bronze ink well and heard a rustling of wings to his right. An angel seemed to come to his ear and dictate . . . .*

(Reprinted by permission of Faber and Faber Ltd)

Kazantzakis presumed:
1 that the Gospel was written by Matthew the Apostle,
2 that his aim was to write a straightforward biography of Jesus,
3 that an angel told him what to write.

The novelist was relying on centuries of Christian tradition. Present-day scholars are very dubious about that tradition, and question all three of Kazantzakis's assumptions.

So, who is Matthew and what sort of book is his Gospel?

What Is a Gospel?

It isn't a biography. It isn't a straightforward account of the life of Jesus of Nazareth. Kazantzakis's novel gives the wrong impression when it portrays Matthew as a man anxious to record historical events for posterity.

In reality, Matthew the writer was less interested in the historical details of Jesus' life than in the total impact Jesus had made on his followers.

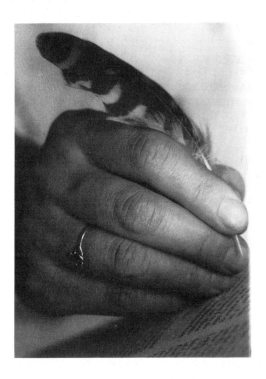

Writing over 40 years after Jesus' death, he was overwhelmed by the 'resurrection' experience. The early Christian community felt that, in Jesus, God had shown himself to be close at hand and present in their very ordinary lives. Since that presence of God remained with them even after Jesus had died, they believed that Jesus' life and victorious death was *The* 'Good News' for all time.

The word 'Gospel' means 'good news'. In the years immediately after Jesus' death his followers spread the news by word of mouth. This preached message was known as the *kerygma* (Greek). It was a proclamation of faith in Jesus. Its content can be gathered from accounts given in the Acts of the Apostles of the preaching of Peter and Paul (see chapters 2, 3, 7 and 10 of Acts).

A summary of the kerygma

God had brought all history to fulfilment.
The life of Jesus of Nazareth showed him to be God's promised Messiah.
He died as God had foretold.
God raised him from the dead and placed him at his right hand.
He will come to save those who accept him as saviour.
Repent and be baptized.

After some time, collections of sayings were written down and then used to expand the kerygma into the Gospels as we know them. Mark, Matthew, Luke and John each elaborated this message in his own way. The four writers are called *Evangelists*, which means people who spread good news.

The first three Gospels—of Mark, Matthew and Luke—obviously depend on the same collection of stories and sayings. Although they were written at different times and in different styles, there is a certain family likeness about them. So they are known as the *Synoptic* (look alike) *Gospels*.

Mark, symbolized by the winged lion

Who Is this Matthew?

After careful research into the writing of the 4 Gospels, most scholars now believe that they were written in this order:

Mark	not before AD65
Matthew	not before AD75
Luke	not before AD85
John	not before AD95.

But we don't really know who the author of 'Matthew' is. It is obvious that he wrote with Mark's Gospel in front of him. In places he has copied it word for word. It is most unlikely that an apostle who had seen the events he wrote about would copy them from someone who hadn't seen them. An eye-witness would have written his own book.

Scholars also deduce from the style of the writing that the unknown author was a Jewish Christian. He may have been a converted rabbi or scribe.

Matthew, symbolized by the divine man

What Sources Did He Use?

1 We've already seen that Matthew the author relied on Mark's Gospel. He repeated 606 of Mark's 661 verses.
2 He added long discourses—the Gospel is almost twice as long as Mark's. Some of this additional material is also in Luke. A few scholars think that Luke copied Mark and Matthew. But most have concluded that Matthew and Luke had access to another document (now lost) which recorded the sayings of Jesus. It is known as the Q document.
3 Matthew's Gospel has about 300 verses which aren't found any-where else. They are known as M—for 'Special to Matthew'.

It is of course possible that Q or M were the work of the actual apostle Matthew, who as a tax-collector would have been an educated man. This could explain the very early tradition that put his name to the whole Gospel. The truth lies hidden from us today.

Luke, symbolized by the winged ox

John, symbolized by the eagle

Matthew's Gospel

Why did Kazantzakis speak of an angel dictating the Gospel to Matthew? It is his way of expressing the Christian belief that the Gospel is the 'word of God'. Christians today would not easily use such a dramatic image. They recognize that a Gospel, like every book of the Bible, is the result of human effort and talent. Nonetheless, when they read these human professions of faith, they claim to hear God speaking to them.

Matthew uses his human talents to express what Jesus' life and teaching mean to him. His Gospel is an invitation to his readers to see Jesus as he saw him. His understanding of Jesus can be broken down into four areas:

1   Jesus is the new Moses, teaching the **New Law**. He does not replace the Old Testament law but brings it to perfection.
2   Jesus is the great teacher **Prophet**. He taught in words and deeds.
3   Jesus is the fulfilment of **Promise**. He is the deliverer promised by the Old Testament.
4   The true Israel is now to be found in the Christian **Community**.

We will look closely at this understanding of Jesus in the four parts of this book.

Questions

The Law

A1 The Law

A collage, called LAW, by an art student. How would you have represented LAW?

Rules and regulations are part of life. Even your family has to have rules and guidelines. They set a pattern which enables you to live together as a community without too much chaos. But mention 'rules' and most people groan. They want to be free from constraint. How many home and school regulations would you like to abandon? What would happen if you did?

The Jewish people have a rather different response to law.

> *The Law you have uttered is more precious to me than all the wealth in the world.*
> Psalm 119:72

> *How I love your Law!*
> *I ponder it all day long.*
> Psalm 119:97

For Jews, the Law is not a burden but a joy. Their Law is found in the first 5 books of the Old Testament (the Pentateuch) and is known as the *Torah*. This word means something like 'guide for living'. The writings contain pieces of legislation but also stories of the Jewish ancestors. The stories combine with the laws to form the respected guide to living for all Jews.

The Torah scroll is handwritten and is so highly respected that it is kept in the most important part of the synagogue—the 'ark' or central 'tabernacle', before which a lamp always burns. When it is brought out and carried round the congregation at a service, the people lean out of their seats to touch it. It is revered as the very presence of God among his people.

A2 Moses and the Law

Some of the stories in the Torah describe Moses' close relationship with God. Abraham is revered as the original ancestor of the Jewish people, but Moses is their greatest teacher. He holds a unique place in Jewish thinking, for upon him the Jewish *Faith* was founded.

> There has never been a prophet in Israel like Moses; the Lord spoke with him face to face. Deuteronomy 34:10

Moses is the central personality in the Pentateuch. It was in his experience of God that Jews came to know the One God. The story of the Jewish people reaches a climax in chapter 20 of the Book of Exodus. Moses is 'face to face with God' on Mount Sinai. He lays down the basic rules for the orderly government of a human society which we know as The Ten Commandments. He tells the people, 'This is how God wants you to live.'

The Ten Commandments (Decalogue) are echoed in other ancient codes. On the 1700BC stele (stone) of Hammurabi, the Babylonian king is depicted receiving his laws from the sun-god Shamash, the god of justice. Moses lived over 400 years later and is also depicted receiving the law from God—the One God whose rules reveal his will for the Chosen People.

> Read Exodus 20:1–20

The Jewish people (Israelites) accepted these Ten Commandments as the terms on which they entered into an agreement, a *covenant* with God. If they lived by these laws, he would protect them. The laws were inscribed on stone and placed in an ark to remain as the permanent record of this covenant.

People throughout the ages have admired these rules of behaviour. They are a concise summary of fundamental principles without which community life is impossible. They ring true, like maker's instructions. The Book of Exodus expresses this by saying they were God's own work.

> When God finished speaking to Moses on Mount Sinai, he gave him the two stone tablets on which God himself had written the Commandments.
> Exodus 31:18

But they are obviously capable of elaboration and interpretation. The later books of the Torah did just that. And the Jewish rabbis (teachers) continued to interpret the Law to meet the needs of their contemporary audiences.

Matthew presents Jesus as *the* Rabbi, the new Moses, who gives a final interpretation to the Law.

A3 The Shema

For the Jews, the Law of God is summed up in a few verses of the book of Deuteronomy. They are known as the *Shema*. All Jewish children learn them by heart as their first prayer, and they continue to be recited daily as part of morning and evening family prayer. They also occur frequently in public synagogue prayer.

> *Hear O Israel (Shema Yisrael), the Lord is our God, the Lord is One.*
> *Love the Lord your God with all your heart, and all your soul, and all your might. These words that I command you today shall be upon your heart. Repeat them to your children, and talk about them when you sit in your home, and when you walk in the street; when you lie down, and when you rise up. Hold fast to them as a sign upon your hand, and let them be as reminders before your eyes. Write them on the doorposts of your home and at your gates.*
>
> Deuteronomy 6:4–9 (Jewish Prayer Book)

Devout Jews have taken the last sentence quite literally. They have written out the Shema, placed it in a case called a *mezuzah*, and fixed it on the doorpost of their homes. This is the service of dedication.

> 'We fix the mezuzah to the doorpost of this home to fulfil the command of our creator and to remind ourselves and all who enter that we should love him with all our heart and all our soul and all our might.
> We ask his blessing on this home and all who live in it. May its doors be open to those in need and its rooms be filled with kindness. May love dwell within its walls, and joy shine from its windows. May his peace protect it and his presence never leave it.
> Blessed are you Lord our God, king of the universe, who makes us holy through doing his commands, and commands us to fix the mezuzah.'

The photo shows a Jew ready for prayer. Bound around his left arm and his head are leather bands each holding small black boxes called *phylacteries*. They contain parchment scrolls on which the Shema and other texts are written. He also wears the fringed prayer shawl (*tallith*) demanded by an instruction in the Book of Numbers (15:37–41).

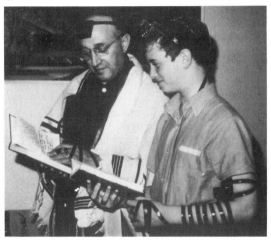

The mezuzah, phylacteries and tallith are outward religious symbols of the words of the Shema. They express the people's love for the loving God who is close to his people.

The Shema was written 600 years after Moses died. The author of the book in which it appears (Deuteronomy = Repetition of the Law) dramatically represents Moses as speaking to a later generation that had been unfaithful to the original covenant Moses had made at Mount Sinai. He sums up the meaning of that covenant:

God has shown his love for you.

Your response must be a loving one.

Matthew presents Jesus as the one whose life was a perfect expression of that love.

Questions and Things to Do

A What do you know?

1 What is the Torah?

2 Give another name for the first five books of the Old Testament.

3 Where in the synagogue is the Torah scroll kept?

4 Who is the original ancestor of the Jewish people?

5 What happened at Mount Sinai?

6 What is a 'covenant'?

7 What does the word 'Shema' mean?

8 What is a 'mezuzah' and where is it kept?

9 What is a 'phylactery'?

10 In which book of the Bible is the Shema to be found?

B Something to do

1 The mezuzah and phylacteries are symbols. What other religious symbols can you think of? Make a list of symbols used in your place of worship.

For Discussion

A great teacher of the Law, Rabbi Hillel (died AD10), was once asked to sum up the whole Jewish Law. He said: 'Don't do to anyone what you would hate being done to you. The rest is commentary.'
A few years later Jesus said:
'Do for others what you want them to do for you: this is the meaning of the Law of Moses and of the teachings of the prophets.'   (Matthew 7:12)

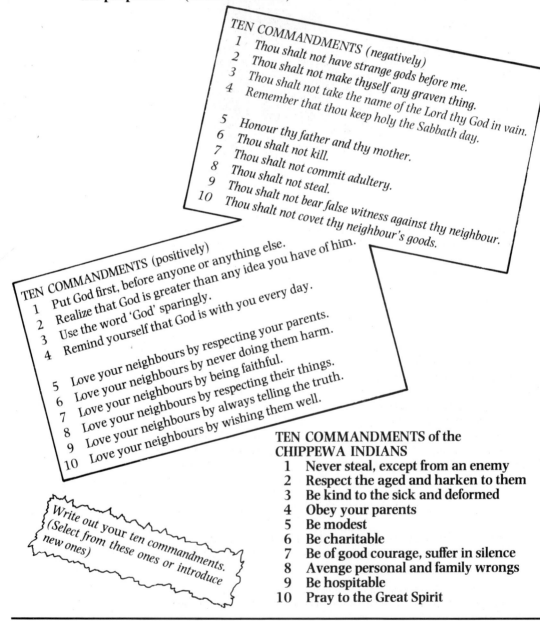

TEN COMMANDMENTS (negatively)
1 Thou shalt not have strange gods before me.
2 Thou shalt not make thyself any graven thing.
3 Thou shalt not take the name of the Lord thy God in vain.
4 Remember that thou keep holy the Sabbath day.
5 Honour thy father and thy mother.
6 Thou shalt not kill.
7 Thou shalt not commit adultery.
8 Thou shalt not steal.
9 Thou shalt not bear false witness against thy neighbour.
10 Thou shalt not covet thy neighbour's goods.

TEN COMMANDMENTS (positively)
1 Put God first, before anyone or anything else.
2 Realize that God is greater than any idea you have of him.
3 Use the word 'God' sparingly.
4 Remind yourself that God is with you every day.
5 Love your neighbours by respecting your parents.
6 Love your neighbours by never doing them harm.
7 Love your neighbours by being faithful.
8 Love your neighbours by respecting their things.
9 Love your neighbours by always telling the truth.
10 Love your neighbours by wishing them well.

TEN COMMANDMENTS of the CHIPPEWA INDIANS
1 Never steal, except from an enemy
2 Respect the aged and harken to them
3 Be kind to the sick and deformed
4 Obey your parents
5 Be modest
6 Be charitable
7 Be of good courage, suffer in silence
8 Avenge personal and family wrongs
9 Be hospitable
10 Pray to the Great Spirit

Write out your ten commandments.
(Select from these ones or introduce new ones)

A4 Jesus and the Law

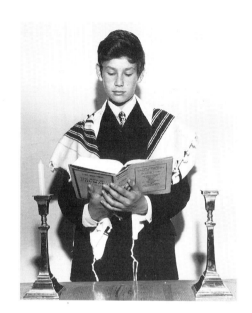

He was a Jewish child,
he had a Jewish nose,
he read the Jewish bible
and wore all Jewish clothes.

He kept the Jewish Law
with Jewish thoroughness,
his Jewish mamma wouldn't let
her Jewish boy do less.

He loved the Jewish feasts,
the Jewish Temple too;
he prayed the Jewish psalter,
a proud and Jewish Jew.

Peter de Rosa, the author of this poem, deliberately put the word 'Jewish' into every line to emphasize for Christians where their roots are. Jesus was a Jew. What he believed and preached was an echo of everything that is deepest in the Jewish faith. Like Rabbi Hillel, who lived only a few years before him, Jesus was a brilliant teacher who could sum up the whole of Jewish Law in a clear and memorable saying or story.

The Evangelist Matthew also emphasizes the Jewishness of Jesus. Just as the Old Testament writers put a number of discourses into the mouth of Moses, Matthew collects together elements of Jesus' teachings, and presents them in five great discourses. We are not to think of Jesus delivering long sermons, or speaking non-stop through a double-period lesson.

It is simply Matthew's way of saying:

Jesus is the new *Moses*.

Matthew's first discourse is very carefully constructed. It is important to Christians because it is a sort of manual of instruction on what it means to believe in Jesus as the Messiah. This section of the Gospel (Matthew 5–7) is known as

> ## The Sermon on the Mount

Jesus proclaims his Law on a mountain, as Moses did. Matthew is reminding his readers that this new Law remains rooted in Judaism. He represents Jesus as saying:

Do not think that I have come to do away with the Law of Moses and the teachings of the prophets. I have not come to do away with them, but to make their teachings come true.   Matthew 5:17

A5 The Sermon on the Mount

*Happy are those who know they are spiritually
poor;
the Kingdom of heaven belongs to them!
Happy are those who mourn;
God will comfort them!
Happy are those who are humble;
they will receive what God has promised!
Happy are those whose greatest desire is to do what
God requires;
God will satisfy them fully!
Happy are those who are merciful to others;
God will be merciful to them!
Happy are the pure in heart;
they will see God!
Happy are those who work for peace;
God will call them his children!
Happy are those who are persecuted because they
do what God requires;
the Kingdom of heaven belongs to them!*

Matthew 5 : 3–10

How on earth could anyone call a woman like this happy. Yet that,
according to Matthew, is what Jesus called her.

Jesus always surprised people by seeming to turn values upside down.
The really lucky people are the poor, the unimportant, the hungry, the
heartbroken, the persecuted.

Why?

Because they are the most qualified to enter God's Kingdom. Rich and
powerful people can easily be self-sufficient. Poor and persecuted people
can't. Their hands are empty—and therefore ready to receive all God's
gifts.

They are, in fact, like Jesus himself, who totally identified with the
outcasts of society.

Matthew opens his discourse with the Eight 'Beatitudes' or Blessings,
which describe the ideal candidates for the Kingdom of God (he uses the
term Kingdom of 'heaven' because devout Jews were reticent about
using the word 'God').

The Beatitudes don't promise eight different rewards for eight different
virtues. They are eight ways of saying the same thing, in the repetitive
style of Jewish poetry. The teaching that follows simply opens out this
first memorable statement of what it means to be a disciple of Jesus.

Read Matthew 5 : 17–48

Son of Man is the title of a controversial television play written by Dennis
Potter. Herbert Kretzmer, a critic, wrote:

> *The play's impact is often brutal. I believe that it says more about the essence of
> Christianity than sermons preached from a dozen pulpits.*

Kretzmer may well have had in mind Potter's scene of the Sermon on the Mount.

Jesus reminds the audience of the Old Testament Law and is urged on by his excited apostles, who are unaware of the sarcasm in Jesus' voice.

Love your ememies . . .
love the soldier . . .

Jesus: An eye for an eye! A tooth for a tooth!
Peter: Hit them hard!
James: Hit them fast!
Jesus: A life for a life!
Andrew: Bone for bone!
John: Muscle for muscle!
Peter: Sword for sword!
Jesus: Kick for kick!
John: Blow for blow!
Andrew: Sting for sting!
Peter: Head for head!
James: Corpse for corpse!
Jesus: An eye for an eye. A tooth for a tooth.
*   Is that not so? Is that not our way?*
Four Disciples: Yes! Yes!
Jesus: Yes! So our forefathers have spoken.
*   . . . . . And they have also said love your kinsman—right?*
*   Makes sense! Love your compatriot. Love your own kind. And HATE the*
*   enemy. HATE-your-enemy.*
*   Right?*
Four Disciples: HATE!

Jesus then paints a picture of cosy and smug people being very nice to one another, to their own kind. When his audience is carried along in this wave of enthusiasm for loving the loveable, Jesus stops. Silence. Then he says the unthinkable.

Love your enemies! Yes. I say it again. Love your enemies. Love—the hardest, toughest, most challenging, most invincible FORCE of all. Love your enemies. Love those who hate you. Love those who would destroy you. Love the man who would kick you and spit at you. Love the soldier who drives the sword into your belly. Love your enemies. We MUST love one another, or we must die.

Read Matthew chapter 5 again. If you have heard the words many times before, they may have lost their impact. Dennis Potter's paraphrase heightens the drama of Jesus' original demands. Potter's Jesus says: 'Oh, I tell you it is hard to follow me.'

Comment on the text

Matthew's readers had great respect for the Law. Matthew tells them to look to Jesus as the one who expresses the *spirit* of the Law. He is criticizing some of the Scribes (teachers) and Pharisees (see page 25) who interpreted the Mosaic Law too woodenly, letter by letter, and so failed to see its deeper meaning.

Chapter 5 presents Jesus as a rabbi interpreting the Law. Even his *style* is rabbinical. He makes a statement:

> *I tell you, then, that you will be able to enter the Kingdom of heaven only if you are more faithful than the teachers of the Law and the Pharisees in doing what God requires.*   Matthew 5:20

Then he applies it to a number of different cases:

---

1   *Read 5:21–26*

On **Anger**: You've heard the commandment 'Do not commit murder'. Well, I say this means don't even get *angry* with your neighbour.

---

2   *Read 5:27–30*

On **Adultery**: You've heard the commandment 'Do not commit adultery'. Well, I tell you this includes committing adultery of the heart just by *looking* at someone lustfully.

---

3   *Read 5:31–32*

On **Divorce**: You've heard it said that anyone can get a legal divorce. Well I tell you that you can't divorce your wife for *any* reason other than for her unfaithfulness.

---

4   *Read 5:33–37*

On **Oaths**: You've heard it said that people should confirm their promises on oath. Well, I say that people who love the truth don't need oaths at all.

---

5   *Read 5:38–42*

On **Revenge**: You've heard it said 'An eye for an eye'. Well I say, not even that; take *NO* revenge at all.

---

6   *Read 5:43–48*

On **Enemies**: You've heard it said, 'Love your friends' as if that entitled you to hate your enemies. Well, I say love your *enemies* too.

These six examples all call for a deep love of neighbours. The first four call for a deeper sensitivity towards others. The last two are even more demanding, and indicate the universal scope of the law of love.

When Jesus uses the phrase 'You've heard it said', he was taking up a formula used by all rabbis to quote what the authorities said on any topic. Typically he does not leave it at that. He adds his own interpretation, on his *own* authority, and claims to put his finger on the *original* meaning of the Law of Moses. This is a call to love others as perfectly as God does.

You must be perfect—just as your Father in heaven is perfect.

In other words

You must set *no* limit on your love, just as God puts none on his.

Questions and Things to Do

A   What do you know?

1   When did Rabbi Hillel die?

2   Write down as many of the Ten Commandments as you can remember.

3   In what way are the first four commandments distinct from the other six?

4   How many great discourses does Matthew present?

5   What is the name given to chapters 5–7 of Matthew?

6   Which two groups of people are criticized by Jesus in chapter 5 : 20?

7   What are the six examples Jesus comments on in chapter 5?

8   For what one reason does Matthew's Jesus allow divorce?

9   What does Jesus say about taking revenge?

10   Finish this quotation: 'You must be perfect . . . .

B   What do you understand?

1   Why does Matthew use the term 'Kingdom of heaven' and not 'Kingdom of God'?

2   Why does Matthew place Jesus' first discourse on a mountain?

3   In what way was Jesus' teaching (in chapter 5) revolutionary?

4   Essay. 'Jesus didn't say " The Law of Moses was imperfect. This is the New Law. Follow me and be a Christian!" He was a Jew, and remained a Jew. He simply said "This is what the Law of Moses really means".' Comment.

C   What do you think?

1   Using examples from today's world, show just how demanding Jesus' teaching is. Do you think it is possible to achieve such perfection?

2   Matthew presents Jesus as a rabbi speaking with great personal authority. What does the word 'authority' mean to you? Describe one (living or recently dead) person who you think had great personal authority. Say why.

D   Something to do

1   Invite a rabbi to talk to you about the Law.

2   Get copies of Dennis Potter's *Son of Man* and act out the Sermon on the Mount scene.

3   Illustrate the Ten Commandments (positive interpretation page 10) using photos and newspaper cuttings. Make it into a wall mural.

4   Find pictures or newspaper reports to illustrate Jesus' teaching in Matthew chapter 5. An example is shown at the foot of the page.

Ireland: Services for forgiveness and healing

On Good Friday this year, services for forgiveness and healing in Ireland and England were held in Belfast, Dublin and London. They took place simultaneously and were each followed by a silent procession. *Joe O'Boyle*, one of the organisers, writes about the London event.

FROM JUST BEHIND the altar in Westminster Abbey, where I was helping to hold upright the carefully prepared wooden cross, dedicated in Derry and sent specially for the London Good Friday service of Reconciliation, Repentance and Forgiveness, I could sense unmistakenly the packed-to-capacity crowd's unity of identification and my own reaction to this time of healing and heartfelt intercession as each of three confession

Jesus interpreted the Law of Moses for his contemporaries. Christian Churches try to interpret the teaching of Jesus for the contemporary world. In some cases their interpretations differ, because the texts remain ambiguous. Discuss these two examples of Jesus' teaching.

1 On marriage

All Christian denominations agree that Jesus upheld the sacredness of marriage. Some even include marriage among the sacraments. But even those who don't go that far stress the solemnity of this commitment, undertaken before God, and blessed by the Church.

The New Testament teaching on marriage seems to take two things for granted:

1 *monogamy (one partner only). See 1 Corinthians 7 : 2–4.*

2 *marriage for life. Paul, Mark (see 10 : 6–9) and John imply that Jesus forbade divorce on any grounds.*

Matthew, in the text we have seen (5 : 32), presumes that divorce is allowed for unfaithfulness. It is, therefore, not surprising that Christian denominations make different conclusions about divorce. The Roman Catholic Church does not recognize civil divorce. The Orthodox and Protestant churches are less absolute in their practice.

Discuss

2 On forgiving others

All Christian denominations agree on the interpretation of Matthew 5 : 38–48. Jesus taught that forgiveness is the proof of true godliness. God forgives totally. Jesus says be God-like in your love for those who hurt you. Roman Catholics express their belief in this fundamental teaching by celebrating God's forgiveness in the sacrament of penance. But . . . . It is not so easy to put into practice.

DISCUSS forgiveness in the light of situations of unrest, injustice or hatred.

A6 The Sermon on the Mount

Blessed are they that mourn: for they
shall be comforted.

The mother of a terrorist will be comforted.
The father of an innocent child will be
comforted.
The wife and children of a policeman
will be comforted.
The wives and mothers of murdered
British soldiers will be comforted.
The families of all those killed in the
bombings will be comforted.
The innocent office workers with perman-
ently scarred faces will be comforted.
The amputees will be comforted.

But Lord, we who read about it, and see
it on television, will you comfort us?

From Ulster O.V. by John Stewart.
Castle Press Limited, Belfast.

IRA VICTIM'S MOTHER IN PLEA TO STOP VIOLENCE

I forgive my son's killers

by JAMES HASTINGS

THE mother of one of the three British servicemen murdered by the IRA in Holland said this week she forgave her son's killers.

Mrs Josephine Baxter said she did not feel hatred or bitterness. "That is how I feel at the moment and I pray our Blessed Lady will give me strength to always feel like that," she said at the family Glasgow home.

Senior Aircraftsman John Baxter, 21, died with his best friend Senior Aircr___

Reid, 22, when a bomb exploded beneath __ car at Nieuw-Bergen in Holla__

Mrs Baxter's family __ speak to othe_ feeli__

Be God-like in your love for those who hurt you

Religious Practice

Chapter 6 of Matthew is a continuation of the Sermon on the Mount. Matthew again brings together pieces of Jesus' teaching to emphasize a particular point. Here he concentrates on religious practice. The general theme is the contrast between deeds done for outward show and those done secretly out of genuine love of God.

Again, in rabbinical style, Jesus gives the general principle and then applies it to the three classical good works of
almsgiving, prayer and fasting.

> Read Matthew 6:1–18

Make certain you do not perform your religious duties in public so that people will see what you do. If you do these things publicly, you will not have any reward from your Father in heaven. Matthew 6:1

Notice how, in applying this principle, Jesus uses the same formula three times.

1 Almsgiving

'When you give something to a needy person,
do not make a big show of it . . . .
But when you help a needy person,
do it in such a way that even your
closest friend will not know about it.
And your Father . . . will reward you,'

2 Prayer

'When you pray,
do not be like the hypocrites . . .
who pray
so that everyone will see them.
But when you pray, . . .
close the door . . . .
And your Father . . . will reward you.

3 Fasting

When you fast,
do not put on a sad face . . .
When you go without food,
wash your face and comb your hair, so that
others cannot know that you are fasting.
And your Father . . . will reward you.

'Our Father in heaven'

Matthew introduces the Lord's Prayer at this point.

It interrupts the general theme but he wants to keep Jesus' comments on prayer together.

Luke also has a simple version of this prayer—also placed in an artificial setting.

Matthew's version is more developed, and sounds as if it had been added to by the early Church for liturgical use.

It has become the prayer which unites all Christian denominations.

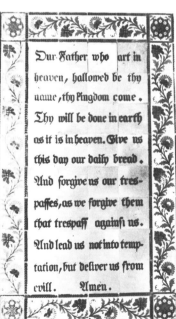

Our Father who art in heaven, hallowed be thy name, thy kingdom come. Thy will be done in earth as it is in heaven. Give us this day our daily bread. And forgive us our trespasses, as we forgive them that trespass against us. And lead us not into temptation, but deliver us from evill. Amen.

Possessions

Matthew continues this section with a collection of sayings which refer back to the earlier part of the chapter. The connecting theme is trust in God and single-mindedness in serving him.

> Read Matthew 6 : 19–34

1   Riches in heaven:

'Do not store up riches . . . on earth . . . Store up riches for yourself in heaven.'

Unworldliness.

2   The light of the body:

'If your eyes are sound, your whole body will be full of light.'

Look in the right direction, ie. Godwards.

3   God and possessions:

1   'You cannot serve both God and money.'

Get your priorities right.

2   'Do not start worrying "Where will my food come from? or my drink? or my clothes?" Your Father in heaven knows that you need all these things.'

Trust in God. He is a Father.

Did Jesus really say all these things?

Scripture scholars try to discover how the early Gospel writings were put together. Some believe that the early Church was responsible for putting many words on Jesus' lips. Professor Bultmann, for example, suggests that Jesus never spoke the kind of wise sayings recorded in chapter 6 of Matthew. Jesus here speaks like a Teacher of Wisdom, and so reflects the Jewish tradition of putting a collection of wise sayings into the mouth of one person. This tradition is highly developed in the Wisdom literature of the Old Testament, eg. Proverbs and Ecclesiastes.

Some Christians would feel cheated if it could be proved that Jesus didn't *actually say* the words that Matthew puts into his mouth. Others would feel less distressed. The early disciples presumably knew that Jesus taught the ideas these words convey. As long as they interpret his teaching, it does not matter if we no longer have his *actual* words.

A7 Conclusion of the Sermon on the Mount

Do for others what you want them to do for you.

Jesus' instructions end with the brilliant eleven-word summary of the whole Old Testament (already seen on page 10). At first sight it looks like simple common sense: smile at people and they'll smile back; shout at a child and he will raise *his* voice; share your lunch with a friend today and she'll do the same for you another day. But to base *everything* you do on this principle is very demanding.

The Sermon concludes with a series of parables (see page 48). Each is based on a familiar Old Testament image. Each emphasizes *contrast*.

1　The wide road, and narrow gate
2　The rotten tree, and the healthy tree
3　Those who only talk, and those who get on with things
4　The house built on sand, and the house with a rock foundation.

Read Matthew 7 : 24–27

A house built on sand

Matthew's metaphor is an interesting final comment. A Jewish audience would take it for granted that the house built on rock represents those who live in obedience to the Mosaic Law. According to Matthew, it is only those who interpret the Law *as Jesus taught it*, who build on safe foundations. Matthew may have had in mind the final words of the last discourse of Moses.

Read Deuteronomy 30 : 15–20

Today I am giving you a choice between good and evil, between life and death. If you obey the commands of the Lord ... then you will prosper ... But if you disobey and refuse to listen ... you will be destroyed.

A Summary of the Sermon on the Mount

Matthew uses the artificial setting of a long sermon delivered on a mountain. Jesus is presented as the new Moses, the teacher and interpreter of God's Law. Matthew is rather torn because he wants to show his readers that Jesus is in direct *continuity* with Moses and the Old Law (they were converts from Judaism and still emotionally attached to it); and yet everything is *new* because Jesus' interpretation of the Law is unique.

In the Sermon Jesus interprets the Law with great freedom and authority. He constantly reminds his disciples to get their priorities right. And he puts *people* first—before rules and regulations.

Questions and Things to Do

A What do you know?

1 What did Jesus say about alms-giving?

2 What did Jesus say about prayer?

3 What did Jesus say about fasting?

4 What general principle was Jesus illustrating with these three examples?

5 Write out the 'Lord's Prayer' from memory.

6 Complete this quotation: 'Do for others what you . . . .

7 Write out the quotation which tells you that you must look in the right direction, towards God.

8 In what way are the four metaphors (parables) in chapter 7 linked together?

9 What happened to the person who built a house on sand?

10 According to Matthew, to whom did Jesus address this sermon?

B What do you understand?

1 Show how Matthew presents Jesus as a rabbi (using examples from chapter 6 only).

2 Is it certain that Jesus actually spoke the words of the Sermon on the Mount? Explain your answer.

C What do you think?

1 Christian Churches interpret the teaching of Jesus in different ways. Why is this? Do you think this weakens or strengthens the cause of Christianity in today's world?

2 'Forgiveness is the proof of true god-liness'. If Christians believe this, should they forgive everyone—whatever the offence?

3 'Make certain you do not perform your religious duties in public so that people will see what you do.' (Matthew 6:1) Isn't this an argument for not going to church?

D Things to do

Make a list of ten laws you obey. Sort out *why* you obey each one. Is it:

(a) because what the law commands is worthwhile,

(b) because it will help you achieve some-thing,

(c) because otherwise you'll be punished?

Compare your results with the group.

Know your rights before going into battle

Loving thy neighbour is all very well... but how can you do it when they get up your nose? By knowing your legal rights, says Jan Kent, head of the Citizens' Advice Bureau in Gravesend, Kent.

● The owner of a cat *cannot* be held responsible for any damage the animal causes.

● It's *your* responsibility to keep next door's dog out of your garden.

● No one has a right park outside their home — and they can't stop anyone else parking there either.

● Noisy children are *not* a nuisance in the eyes of the law.

● You *can* crop a tree overhanging your garden. But the bits you ʳ off remain your bour's propertʸ'

● You arᵉ confisᶜʳ no

The beginning and the end of the law is kindness (Jewish proverb)

A father complained to the Rabbi that his son had forsaken God.
'What shall I do, Rabbi?'
'Love him more than ever' was his reply.

THE LAW AND YOU

It is the sharing which is under-developed.

neighbours

All Christians are called to act.
For stating principles is not enough.
To point out injustice, not enough.
Prophetic cries are not enough.
Words lack weight unless we all become responsible and act effectively.
(*Octogesima Adveniens* Pope Paul VI)

Draw up a list of Christians who you think base their lives on the command to 'love other people'.

A8 Expansion of the theme

Throughout the Gospel Matthew refers again and again to this theme because of the need to reassure his readers that they are the *True Israel*. Here are six examples of the expanded theme.

Example 1   Put People First

Jesus' interpretation of the Law gets him into conflict with the authorities. In chapters 11 and 12 Matthew highlights the confrontation. There are two incidents in chapter 12 which again illustrate Jesus' *priority for people*.

> Read Matthew 12:1–14

In these two incidents Jesus is challenged by the Pharisees for seeming to break the Law.

'Look, it is against our Law for your disciples to do this on the Sabbath!' 12:2 (to pluck corn and eat it).

'Is it against our Law to heal on the Sabbath?' 12:10. (Jesus heals the man who has a paralyzed hand.)

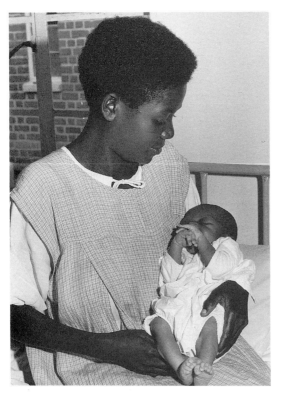

In both stories Jesus insists that he is following the Law. He justifies his actions, using good rabbinic argument. But he goes beyond this to show that formal ritual law has always to give way to the greater law of *love* and human compassion.

Read these two stories as told in Mark 2:23ff and Luke 6:1ff. You'll notice a few differences. Matthew is thinking of his Jewish-Christians when he introduces the Old Testament quotation 'It is kindness that I want, not animal sacrifices'. This recalls the whole Jewish understanding of God's 'kindness', his constant, loving guidance of Israel.

The real followers of the Law are those who act in this godlike way, putting people's needs first.

Putting another person's need first

Example 2   Traditions can Strangle

In this example Matthew points out how laws can be manipulated. Jesus has no time for the observance of law 'to the letter' when the *spirit* of the law is violated.

> *Read Matthew 15 : 1–9*

The Pharisees and teachers of the Law again accuse Jesus. 'Why is it that your disciples disobey the teaching handed down by our ancestors? They don't wash their hands in the proper way before they eat!'

Matthew (rearranging Mark's story to suit his own way of presenting Jesus) has Jesus reply to the accusation by *himself* accusing the Pharisees and teachers of breaking the Law:

'You disregard God's command, in order to follow your own teaching. You hypocrites!'

The reference here is to the Law of *Corban*. A man who had financial obligations to his parents could sign the money over to 'God' instead, and so avoid his obligations! 'Hypocrisy' says Jesus.

Pharisaic traditions like this can't be the Law of God—not if they express selfishness and sin against one's neighbour. Matthew's criterion is again one of *love* of neighbour. That is always the measure of God's Law. The Pharisees are condemned only when they fail in this.

Pharisees and Sadducees

Pharisees have a bad name. Yet they weren't all hypocrites; many welcomed Jesus because his teachings did echo their love of God. They, like Jesus, were the lay people who took the Law of Moses seriously. They followed it meticulously. And like Jesus they defended the Word of God against the wordliness of the professional priests and aristocrats—the Sadducees—who formed the real opposition to Jesus. Matthew made the Pharisees into Jesus' enemy because at the time he wrote they had become the anti-Christian party.

The Teachers of the Law (Scribes)

During the Babylonian Exile, 586BC, with everything else destroyed, the Jewish sacred writings became desperately important. They were collected, copied and edited by Scribes, or writers. (Not everyone could read or write.) Jesus' complaint against these teachers was that when they began to interpret these writings they also began to misinterpret them.

Example 3   The Stone Commandments are not enough

Read Matthew 19:16–30

If you want to be perfect, go and sell all you have and give the money to the poor, and you will have riches in heaven; then come and follow me.

Matthew 19:21

This text has inspired many people, over the centuries, to adopt a specialized form of Christian life. The nun in the photo is one of them. The text is the basis for her vow of poverty. But the Gospel-writers did not have religious life in mind when they included this incident in their writings. It was addressed to everyone. The text applies, just as much, to the Christian family in the second photo.

To be a disciple of Jesus is *demanding*. The story implies the total commitment necessary to follow Jesus. And that means letting go of everything else. It means going beyond the letter of the Law.

The incident of the rich young man is one of the most striking stories in the Gospels. Read it carefully and bear the following points in mind.

1   The man asks what he has to do to receive eternal life. 'Keep the commandments' says Jesus. The man replies that he has obeyed them—to the letter. Then Jesus asks for that extra: 'If you want to be *perfect* (remember Matthew 5:48)...come and follow me.' The following of the Law, letter by letter, is not enough. It is Jesus' interpretation of the Law that has to be followed.

2   Read Mark's version of the opening line (Mark 10:17). Notice where the word 'good' comes. Mark suggests that Jesus could not be called 'God'. Did Matthew reword the text because he disagreed with Mark, or did he simply make an inaccurate copy?

3   Prosperity was considered a sign of God's favour. Jesus' teaching contradicts this. This amazes the disciples.

4   Other texts make it obvious that Jesus didn't despise wealth. (See Matthew 11:18–19.) Life is to be enjoyed and celebrated. But possessions must never get in the way of serving God. 'Your heart will always be where your riches are.'   (Matthew 6:21)

5   Read Mark's list of commandments (Mark 10:19) and notice that Matthew adds one more: 'Love your neighbour as you love yourself.' Once again Matthew is really saying, 'This is what it's all about.'

Example 4   Get Your Priorities Right

As the Gospel story progresses the rift between Jesus and the authorities grows ever wider. Matthew (following Mark) has another group of incidents which show this growing tension. Jesus has arrived in Jerusalem. The final conflict is about to begin.

> *Read Matthew 22:15–22*

The Pharisees and the Herodians join forces and set about trapping Jesus by asking an 'impossible' question on Jewish Law. Should a Jew pay taxes to a pagan Roman Emperor? Did the *Law* allow it? Whichever answer Jesus gave he was going to upset someone.

If *he said* 'Yes, we are part of this political system and should pay our taxes', he would anger the Jewish crowds assembling for the Feast. Many Jews resented the Roman occupation. The extreme wing of the liberation movement was a group calling themselves *Zealots*, and they found some sympathy with the *Herodians*. The Pharisees didn't object to paying taxes to Rome because they saw the benefits that followed, especially to themselves.

If *Jesus said* 'No, we shouldn't pay taxes to Rome, it is contrary to our Law,' he could be accused of being an agitator. That could mean a Roman death sentence.

But Jesus avoided the trap.

1   He asked for a coin. Jewish coins did not have a head featured on them. Those with Tiberius Caesar's head on were minted especially for tax purposes. Jesus didn't have this controversial coin himself. But they had one, even though they pretended to protest against Roman taxation! More hypocrisy!

2   Jesus goes to the heart of the matter. By law, all coins belong to the sovereign stamped on them. Jesus says we must acknowledge this. But it is even more important to acknowledge the image stamped on ourselves. We belong to God.

Herodians

It is not altogether clear who they were. The Herod dynasty existed for 50 years before Jesus, and continued for another 100 years after his death. When Herod the Great died (4BC) the land was divided between his three sons. One of them, Archelaus, was so unpopular that the Jews petitioned his removal from Judaea. So Rome established direct rule. The Herodians were possibly a patriotic party which favoured independence from Rome and wanted a member of Herod's family back on the throne.

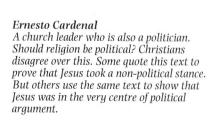

Ernesto Cardenal
A church leader who is also a politician.
Should religion be political? Christians
disagree over this. Some quote this text to
prove that Jesus took a non-political stance.
But others use the same text to show that
Jesus was in the very centre of political
argument.

Example 5   The Law is a Jungle

Read Matthew 22:34–40

The Pharisees make another attempt to catch Jesus out.
'When the Pharisees heard that Jesus had silenced the Sadducees, they came together, and one of them, a teacher of the Law, tried to trap him with a question. "Teacher", he asked, "Which is the greatest commandment in the Law?"'   (Matthew 22:34–36.)

A Jewish lawyer asks this question. There was an ongoing dispute amongst lawyers about the 613 commandments of Law. Which were important and which were unimportant? Jesus is invited to enter the controversy.

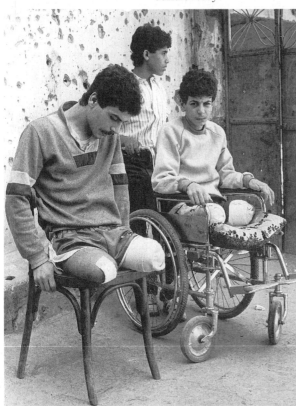

Young victims of war. Hatred of brother implies hatred of God.

He quite simply reminds them of the *Shema* (see page 8). They should have known themselves, from their daily recitation of the prayer, that *the* commandment is to

'Love the Lord your God with all your heart,
with all your soul, and with all your mind.'

But Jesus adds a very significant second commandment which he places not after the first but alongside it.

'Love your neighbour as you love yourself.' (See Leviticus 19:18.)

Jesus' reply is a startling reminder to his critical questioners that the Law is always about *people*—not about rules and regulations, or outward observance and practice.

The wording of verse 39 is important:

'The second most important commandment is like it.'

The two commandments 'Love of God' and 'Love of neighbour' are like each other. Love of God implies love of neighbour. Matthew has insisted all through the Gospel that Jesus sees this as the true interpretation of Mosaic Law.

Writing some years later, John develops this understanding. He wrote:

If someone says he loves God, but hates his brother, he is a liar. For he cannot love God, whom he has not seen, if he does not love his brother, whom he has seen.   1 John 4:20

Matthew places the two commandments alongside each other. John goes further and says they *are* the same thing.

A What do you know?

1 With whom was Jesus often in conflict?

2 Give two incidents when Jesus was accused of breaking the Sabbath.

3 What was wrong with the man whom Jesus healed on the Sabbath?

4 Jesus' disciples were criticized for not washing their hands. How did Jesus reply to the criticism?

5 What is the Law of Corban?

6 When did the office of Scribe (Teacher of the Law) come into prominence?

7 Jesus *named* the commandments for the rich young man. Matthew has one more commandment than Mark. What was it?

8 Which two groups joined forces to trap Jesus on the question of taxation?

9 Which of Herod's sons was deposed?

10 How many commandments of Jewish Law were there?

B What do you understand?

1 Briefly describe why Matthew feels torn when he presents Jesus as a new Moses.

2 Describe the difference between the Pharisees and the Sadducees.

3 Outline the trick question to Jesus about paying tax to Rome. How did Jesus avoid the trap?

4 Outline the teaching of Jesus in the Sermon on the Mount.

5 What, according to Jesus, were the two most important commandments?

C What do you think?

1 Do you think Jesus despised wealthy people? Give Gospel examples to back up your answer.

2 Write an essay showing how Matthew emphasizes an interpretation of the Law which concentrates on *people*, not on rules and regulations.

D Things to do

1 Select five passages from Matthew's Gospel on the theme of Jesus as the new Moses. Find photographs which could illustrate your five texts. Display your work.

'A Conservative MP said in a speech in the House of Commons debate on the air attack made in April 1986 by the United States on Libya: "The Sermon on the Mount undoubtedly set the highest standard of individual behaviour that anyone could require, but it does not apply to those of us in the House who are responsible for the interests of millions of people."'

QUESTION
1   Is Jesus' teaching totally unrealistic?
2   Is there such a thing as a public morality as distinct from a private morality?

THE DEVIL'S BEATITUDES

Blessed are those who are too tired, busy or disorganized to meet with their fellow Christians on Sunday each week—they are my best workers.

Blessed are those who enjoy noticing the mannerisms of clergy, choir and servers—I can see their heart is not in it.

Blessed are the Christians who wait to be asked, and expect to be thanked—I can use them.

Blessed are the touchy—with a bit of luck they can even stop going to Church.

Blessed are those who keep themselves, their time and their money to themselves—they are my missionaries.

Blessed are those who claim to love their God at the same time as hating other people—they are mine forever.

Blessed are the troublemakers—they shall be called my Children.

Blessed are those who have no time to pray—they are easy prey to me.

Blessed are you when you read this and think it is about other people and not about yourself—I've got you.

REFLECTION
Did the devil 'get you'?

Example 6   The Last Word on the Subject

> *Read Matthew 25 : 31–46*

I was hungry and you fed me,
thirsty and you gave me a drink;
I was a stranger and you received me in your homes,
naked and you clothed me;
I was sick and you took care of me,
in prison and you visited me.
The righteous will then answer him, 'When Lord, did we ever see you hungry
and feed you? . . . .'

In this memorable passage Matthew reaches the culmination of the theme that has been central to the Gospel. There is no parallel passage in the other Gospels, and no guarantee that Jesus actually spoke these words. But clearly they do express the vision Jesus had. They also reveal the way Matthew saw Jesus as the mysterious Son of Man, almost indistinguishable from God himself. (See page 83.)

One commentator (Wansbrough) points out that the scene 'is a supreme example of the use and transformation of *Jewish* material.' The story is based on Jewish ideas about the final judgement. But Matthew has introduced three major innovations:

1   In the Jewish scene God is judge;
    in Matthew's story judgement is passed by Jesus as the Son of Man.
2   In the Jewish scene the Gentiles appear only to be condemned;
    in Matthew's story 'all nations' are judged equally.
3   In the Jewish scene people are judged on their good works;
    in Matthew's story the good works are reduced to the *love* of neighbour.

The position of this passage in the Gospel is important. It is Jesus' final word, the end of his fifth great discourse. It therefore sums up Matthew's message to his readers. Jesus, the new Moses, has given the new and final interpretation of the Law. With absolute freedom and authority Jesus simplifies the whole concept of Law. There is only one priority—*people*. Love of God is always expressed by loving people—especially the oppressed and those on the fringes of society.

At this point, Matthew leads straight into the Passion. 'The Son of Man' he says 'will be handed over to be crucified.' Jesus will immediately *himself* identify with the outcasts, the poor and suffering.

Jesus identifies himself with
the refugee

Discussion and Revision

Read Matthew 5:9

'The ultimate weakness of violence is that it is a descending spiral, begetting the very thing it seeks to destroy. Instead of diminishing evil it multiplies it . . . Returning violence for violence multiplies violence . . . Darkness cannot drive out darkness, only light can do that. Hate cannot drive out hate, only love can do that.'

Martin Luther King

Read Matthew 5:9

Read Matthew 5:43

Read Matthew 7:1

'I respect men who, driven by their conscience, decide to use violence—not the cheap violence of the drawing room guerrilla, but the violence of those who have testified to their sincerity by sacrificing their lives. It seems to me that Father Camillo Torres and Che Guevara deserve as much respect as Martin Luther King.'

Helder Camara (Roman Catholic Bishop)

'Do not judge your neighbour until you have stood in his shoes.'

Rabbi Hillel

A proposal was brought to the United Nations that all Scriptures, of all religions, should be revised. Anything which could lead to intolerance, bigotry or cruelty should be deleted. Anything that was against the dignity of people should be dropped. It was revealed that the author of the proposal was Jesus Christ. Reporters rushed to interview him. When asked for an explanation he replied: 'The Scriptures were made for man, not man for the Scriptures.'

Read Matthew 12:1–14

Read Matthew 22:15ff

Read Matthew 22:34ff

Read Matthew 25:31ff

Inland Revenue PAYE

How we work out your tax code

Inland Revenue PAYE–Notice of codin

Please keep this notice for fu reference and let me know o change in your address. The en notes explain the entries.

This notice cancels any previous notice o Your employer or paying officer will use below. Please check this notice. If you think it of appeal. Please let me know at once about an

P3(T)1988   Coding Guide for year to 5 April 1989

'Is it against our law to pay taxes?'
Matthew 22:17

'In the first century of Christianity the hungry were fed at a personal sacrifice, the naked were clothed at a personal sacrifice, the homeless were sheltered at a personal sacrifice.
And because the poor were fed, clothed and sheltered at a personal sacrifice, the pagans used to say about the Christians: "See how they love each other."
In our own day the poor are no longer fed, clothed or sheltered at a personal sacrifice, but at the expense of the taxpayers. And because the poor are no longer fed, clothed and sheltered the pagans say about the Christians: "See how they pass the buck."'
Peter Maurin

'I was hungry and you fed the arms race to protect my "freedom".

I was thirsty and you built armoured tanks instead of clean water tanks.

I was homeless and you built fall-out shelters in your back gardens.

I was naked and you clothed and trained the armed forces.

I was sick but the scientists were too busy perfecting new weapons systems.

I was a prisoner of poverty and you argued that it was because of laziness.

Then it will be the turn of the President and the Generals, and all who were indifferent to ask: "Lord, when did we see you hungry or thirsty, homeless or naked, sick or in prison, and did not come to your help?" Then he will answer, "I tell you most solemnly, in so far as you neglected to do this to one of the least of these, you neglected to do it to me:"'

1 On which text in Matthew is this reading based?
(a) Give the reference (b) Briefly outline the parable. (3)

2 In the Gospel story Matthew uses a Jewish idea of Last Judgement. Give two examples of the way Matthew *changes* the Jewish story. (2)

3 Write a paragraph to show how the Matthew text is related to the theme of the Sermon on the Mount (chapters 5–7). (5)

4 The version of Matthew's text quoted above was written by a supporter of nuclear disarmament. Describe the work of a group which works for world peace OR the relief of poverty/suffering. (5)

5 Comment on the following:
Anne and Eileen are neighbours. Anne doesn't go to any church, but works tirelessly for a human rights group. Eileen has no interest in any social problems. She goes to her church often, and is worried by Anne's lack of religion. Which of the two would you describe as a religious person? (5)

Things to do

1 Write your own version of the Matthew text discussed on this page. Make it into a large, colourful poster.

2 Do some further reading on issues introduced. Make use of places like the Peace Education Resources Centre, 48 Elmwood Avenue, Belfast BT9 6AZ, or Centre for Peace Studies, St Martin's College, Lancaster, or Justice and Peace Resource Centre, 28 Rose Street, Glasgow G3.

Useful reading:

Who is my Neighbour? (CEM, 1982)
Christians as Peacemakers Audrey Kelly (Quaker Peace & Service, 1983)
The Politics of Love John Ferguson (Clarke & Co, 1973)
What the Bible says about Peace John Knox
What the Bible says about Justice Sr Paticia Murray
What the Bible says about Reconciliation Eric Gallagher
   (The above three ICC/ICJP 1978–86)
Prayers for Peacemakers Edited Valerie Flessati   (Kevin Mayhew Publishers, 1988)

Part B

The Prophets

Here .. is the authentic voice of Christian prophecy in our day. Unafraid to proclaim with urgency the truth about apartheid as the evil force it is. Unafraid to risk the consequences for himself of making such a proclamation. But always in hope: always in love: always in the certainty that God is present within the situation.

Bishop Trevor Huddleston, writing about Archbishop Desmond Tutu.

B1   Who are the prophets?

Several classes of pupils preparing for GCSE were asked to name a modern prophet. Three names kept coming up:
Mother Teresa, Archbishop Desmond Tutu and Bob Geldof. Why these three people?

Mother Teresa

For twenty years Mother Teresa was a Loreto nun teaching geography at St Mary's High School in Calcutta. But she was distressed by the contrast between her convent life and the misery of the poor and destitute people sitting on the pavement outside. She left her community to found the Missionaries of Charity. The situation (or as she would say, God) had spoken to her and *called* her to serve them.

Archbishop Desmond Tutu

The Anglican Archbishop of Johannesburg once said: 'I cannot help it when I see injustice. I cannot keep quiet.' He is a voice for the down-trodden and oppressed, especially for his own black people of South Africa. A Roman Catholic priest working in Soweto writes: 'When he speaks in the townships, the people listen with eagerness as if they had not heard him before. He *speaks* with the authority of a prophet.' (Fr Buti Thlagale)

Bob Geldof

Before 1984 Bob Geldof was the leader of the Irish pop group Boomtown Rats. After 1984 and the tragic famine in Ethiopia, he became an international conscience. He saw the scenes of starvation on his television screen, as all the world did. But he acted on what he saw and with a remarkable determination demanded a world-wide response. He *acted* like a prophet.

The Oxford dictionary gives several definitions of the word prophet: 'Inspired teacher, interpreter of God's will; spokesman, advocate (of principle); one who foretells events.'

Most people understand prophecy in this last sense, as a *foretelling* of the future. In actual fact, the Old Testament prophets, though they express great hopes about the future, do very little foretelling. They are much more *forthtellers*, outspoken advocates of God's will here and now.

Mother Teresa, Archbishop Tutu and Bob Geldof are prophets in this sense. They speak out in words and deeds to proclaim a truth which is endangered by people's selfishness and blindness.

The first and greatest of the Old Testament Prophets was Moses. He interpreted to the Israelites the meaning of their exodus from Egypt. It was the moment they became God's Chosen People, bound to him by covenant.

From that time onwards, groups of prophets, then outstanding individuals, tried to keep this vision before Israel's eyes. Israel's prophetical movement began at the time the monarchy was instituted. The books of Samuel and Kings describe a rather primitive and political movement, usually attached to the royal court.

From about 750BC onwards a series of great men emerged from this movement—individuals who championed the covenant made at Sinai, where God had been proclaimed as the only ruler of Israel. Their preaching has been preserved in books of the Old Testament. The major prophets are Isaiah, Jeremiah and Ezekiel.

It is significant to Matthew that Moses is the first and greatest of the prophets. He will naturally want to show his readers that Jesus is, like Moses, the prophet of God.

In this part of the book we will see the ways in which Matthew presents Jesus as a prophet:

the one *called* by God (see page 38),
the one who *speaks* with authority (see page 44),
the one who *acts* in a prophetic manner (see page 54).

Michaelangelo's Moses

B2   Jesus, the one CALLED by God

Throughout the ages individuals have felt *called* to dedicate their lives to a cause or to the service of others. Many people can point to a definite moment of 'calling'. Some will express this in words like:

> 'I knew at that moment what I had to do.'
> 'I knew that God wanted me to do this.'

Mother Teresa knew what she had to do when she saw the destitute people at her gate.

How did the 'call' come to Jesus?

Matthew describes the calling of Jesus in the section of Gospel that precedes the Sermon on the Mount. It is significant that it opens with John the Baptist preaching: 'Turn away from your sins, because the Kingdom of heaven is near!' (Matthew 3:2) It concludes with the same words, but this time from the mouth of Jesus: 'Turn away from your sins, because the Kingdom of heaven is near.' (Matthew 4:17) In the words that lie between these two identical sentences, Matthew describes how Jesus (leaving the obscurity of his home life) came forward to be baptized by John, to be declared God's Son by a voice from heaven, to be tempted in the wilderness and to begin his public ministry. It is the scene of his calling.

It is set in the context of a people needing to turn away from sin, back to a true service of God. Prophets always emerged from similar situations in Israel's history. The prophets describe their call as though God spoke personally to them. It may be that he spoke to them through the situation itself. That was where they heard God's voice.

> Read Amos 7:10–17

> *'The Lord took me from my work as a shepherd and ordered me to come and prophesy to his people Israel.'*

> And read Jeremiah 1:4–10

> *'The Lord said to me, "I chose you before I gave you life, and before you were born I selected you to be a prophet to the nations."'*

So the prophets believed they were destined to be God's spokesmen. It was an unpopular vocation because much of the time their message was that people had to change.

> *'The Lord says, "People of Israel, if you want to turn, then turn back to me."'*   Jeremiah 4:1

Matthew sees John the Baptist as the last in this line of prophets. Then Jesus appears. And he is the fulfilment of all that the prophets hoped for.

B3 Preaching of John the Baptist

Read Matthew 3:1–12

John the Baptist was an important figure of his day. He held a one-man campaign of baptizing all who would come to him. He was clearly seen as a prophet. He dressed in the strange clothes that distinguished Elijah, who (the Old Testament had promised) would return to herald 'the great and terrible day of the Lord's coming'. Matthew believed that John was Elijah returned from heaven (see Matthew 17:10). John's role was to provide the setting for the coming of Jesus as the Messiah.

Matthew and Luke give more detail of John's preaching than Mark. They use the source Q (see page 3) to describe John's preaching about repentance.

There are three points to notice:

1 John comes across as a stern preacher. His message is revolutionary. This is no time for half measures, because the new age is about to break in. The Kingdom of heaven is at hand. Judgement will be passed. Those unfit for the Kingdom will be destroyed, because this judgement is like a raging forest fire. Serpents beware.

2 Luke addresses these words to the multitudes. Matthew picks on the Pharisees and Sadducees as the target. For him, they are the main representatives of unbelief and the wilful rejection of Jesus. Here he has John the Baptist warn them that descent from Abraham will not, of itself, save them from God's wrath. Only faithfulness to the Sinai covenant will do that.

Matthew continues to accuse these two groups of infidelity to the Old Testament (see Matthew 21:33 and page 25). His tone is so condemnatory that later Christians used these texts to justify anti-Semitism (hatred of Jews).

3 Each evangelist points out the superiority of Jesus. He surpasses John who is unworthy to do even the most menial task for him (carry his shoes). John only baptizes with water, but Jesus will baptize with the Holy Spirit and fire. Both of these symbols were used by Old Testament prophets to speak of Judgement Day. Ezekiel, Jeremiah and Isaiah looked forward to the coming of the Spirit to breathe new life into God's people. Malachi spoke of a purifying element more effective than water. On the day of Judgement, God will come 'like a fire that refines metal'. (Malachi 3:3)

B4 The baptism of Jesus

Believer's baptism, Norwich

> Read Mark 1:9–11 and Matthew 3:13–17

Going under the water at baptism is a symbolic act. Candidates are immersed in water as if they are to die by drowning. When they come out again, it is like rising from the dead to new life. This is exactly what John was demanding of the people.

Jesus joins the crowd. According to Mark, he naturally stands alongside his fellow Jews to welcome the coming of the Kingdom.

Matthew seems ill at ease with this account. Maybe he couldn't believe that Jesus needed baptism. It could be that when he was writing there were still some followers of John the Baptist claiming that their prophet hero was superior to Jesus. To disarm them, Matthew says John was reluctant to baptize Jesus.

The event is represented as the turning point in Jesus' life. He was moved by God's Spirit to begin his public ministry. It is the moment he received his calling.

The three synoptic writers describe the scene of the baptism itself in the same way:

God's heaven was opened,
God's Spirit came down,
God's voice was heard.

The images are echoes of the Old Testament. Jesus' baptism was:

1   The answer to Isaiah's cry: 'Why don't you tear the sky apart and come down?' (Isaiah 64:1)
2   A new creation, with God's Spirit again hovering over the waters. (Genesis 1:2)
3   A confirmation that the Messianic age had arrived. The voice from heaven speaks the words which the Book of Isaiah had used to describe the servant of the Lord: 'The one I have chosen, with whom I am pleased.' (Isaiah 42:1)
4   A reminder that the Kingdom was at hand. A kingdom needs a king. At the coronation ceremony the words of Psalm 2 were spoken over the new king: 'You are my son.'

Did Jesus Know He Was the Messiah?

Many Christians assume that Jesus, being the Son of God, always knew exactly what his mission was. Scripture scholars are more reluctant to speculate on Jesus' understanding of his relationship to God, or of his role as Messiah. They remind us that when we read Matthew's Gospel we are being told what Matthew thought about Jesus, not necessarily what Jesus thought about himself. That remains unclear.

B5   The temptation of Jesus

Read Matthew 4:1–11

After his baptism, Jesus is led by the Spirit to the desert to be 'tempted'. This word might suggest that he was being enticed into doing something wrong. But in Jewish terms the word means 'tested', and this was a mark of God's favour. Anyone who survives such a trial emerges strengthened and purified.

Mark mentions this trial in a single sentence. Matthew elaborates. The scene can be looked at on two levels.

1 *The scriptural level.* Jesus' test is modelled on the testing of the people of Israel in the desert after the exodus from Egypt. They wandered for forty years. Jesus remains forty days under his trial. Each of Jesus' replies to his three temptations is a quotation from the book of Deuteronomy.

Israel was tested and often failed. Jesus was tested and remained faithful to God.

2 *The psychological level.* Jesus, like anyone undertaking a new mission, needs time to think. He reflects on all the possibilities, and rejects the comfortable, superficial and attractive aspects of his role. That's the Devil's way, not God's.

1st Temptation   (Hunger for bread)

When the Israelites crossed the Sea of Reeds, they were hungry and longed to return to the flesh-pots of Egypt (Exodus 16). God, in his faithful love, fed them on manna. Commenting on this scene, Deuteronomy said; 'Man must not depend on bread alone to sustain him, but on everything that the Lord says' (Deuteronomy 8:3, much as Jesus said in Matthew 4:4).

2nd Temptation   (The demand of a sign of God's power)

Even after the gift of manna, the Israelites complained and demanded water. They assumed they could make such demands on their God. God did provide water but named the place 'Testing' and 'Complaining'. Jesus does not try to manipulate God like this. He uses the same words in Matthew 4:7 as the author of Deuteronomy reflecting on the scene: 'Do not put the Lord your God to the test' (Deuteronomy 6:16).

3rd Temptation   (Political messiahship)

According to Deuteronomy, Moses promised the people a land with 'large and prosperous cities'. But he told them not to get carried away by earthly things. 'Honour the Lord your God, worship only him' (Deuteronomy 6:10–13). Jesus reiterates this when all the kingdoms are set out before him for the taking (Matthew 4:10).

For Matthew, Jesus is the new Moses, the faithful leader of the new Israel. He will lead the people into the Kingdom of heaven.

Questions and Things to Do

A What do you know?

1 Who was the first and greatest Old Testament prophet?

2 When did the 'prophetical movement' begin in Israel?

3 Name two major prophets.

4 In what way was John the Baptist related to Jesus?

5 Who said: 'Turn away from your sins, because the Kingdom of heaven is near'?

6 Which prophet was expected to return to herald the Lord's coming?

7 To whom does Matthew address John the Baptist's words about judgement?

8 Name the two symbols used in the Old Testament to speak about Judgement Day.

9 What were the three 'temptations' Jesus underwent?

10 From which Old Testament book were his answers to the Devil taken?

B What do you understand?

1 In what way is Archbishop Tutu a prophet?

2 Explain the statement 'prophecy is more about forthtelling than about foretelling'.

3 Explain in a paragraph the tone of John the Baptist's preaching.

4 Why is a prophet's vocation an unpopular one?

5 In what way is *water* a symbol at baptism?

6 Show how the images used in the baptism scene are echoes of Old Testament longing.

7 Outline the three temptations of Jesus and say how they were related to the Old Testament exodus story.

C What do you think?

1 Write a paragraph about someone you would regard as a prophet. Say why you chose him/her.

2 How do you think God speaks to people

(a) in actual words you could put on tape?

(b) in their mind and imagination?

(c) in the situation and events of their lives?

Say why you make your choice and give examples.

3 Some Christians believe that Jesus always knew exactly where he was going. Others believe he only slowly and gradually realized his mission in life. Which view do you take? Say why.

4 In what way is Christian baptism related to Jesus' baptism by John? What is to be said for and against the baptism of infants?

D Some things to do

1 Find out more about the actual practice of the sacrament of baptism in different Christian churches.

2 (a) Invite someone who has experienced a religious calling to come and talk to you.

(b) Compare this experience with other adults who have felt 'called' to a profession or way of life (eg. an artist).

BAPTISM
Going under the water at baptism is
a symbolic act. (See page 40.)

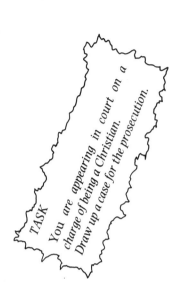

TASK
You are appearing in court on a
charge of being a Christian.
Draw up a case for the prosecution.

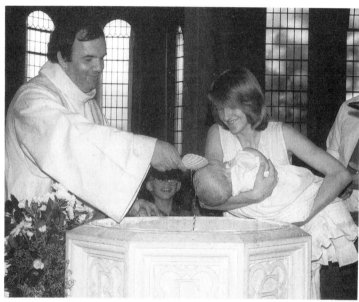

'Friends of Jesus think of how he was
"drowned" in suffering till he died, and how
they want to join Jesus there in order to be
rescued by God, and live a new life. A person
who is baptized says, as Jesus said,
"I would die for God if I had to."'

(*The Sacraments for Children* H J Richards)

'Friends of Jesus who have been confirmed
are called witnesses of Jesus. Looking at them,
people should be able to say,
"Now I understand what Jesus is about."'
(*The Sacraments for Children* H J Richards)

CONFIRMATION
Most Christians are baptized as
babies. When they are older they are
asked if they want to 'confirm' their
baptism.

Confirmation group from Londonderry

B6 Jesus, the one who Speaks with authority

An Orthodox bishop was invited to speak at a Catholic theological conference. The subject under discussion was 'sin'. A Catholic theologian gave a brief outline of his Church's traditional distinction between venial and mortal sins. 'Venial sin is the easily forgiveable wrongdoing of everyday life. It is cheating, pride, spitefulness. It is loving ourselves much more than we love others. But mortal sin is deadly. It is so serious that it cuts the person off from God altogether.'

The Orthodox bishop was invited to say how he regarded this distinction between venial and mortal sin. This is what he said. 'I was a doctor at a field hospital during the war. A soldier was brought in, peppered with bullets and losing a lot of blood. He survived because the bullets hadn't penetrated any vital organ. The same day another soldier was carried in. He was in a high fever. He had cut his finger on a tin of rations. He died.'

This is the West meeting the East. The Western theologian made his point in abstract language. Typically, the Easterner made his point by telling a story.

West meeting East in prayer at Assisi

Jesus was an Easterner. He told stories. Stories are powerful; they capture the imagination and remain in the memory. The stories which Jesus told are called *parables*. Jesus' teaching was about the Kingdom of heaven. According to Matthew his whole preaching career began with this message, 'Turn away from your sins, because the Kingdom of heaven is near.' (Matthew 4:17)

B7 Parables

When Jesus' disciples asked him to explain the basic qualification for becoming members of the Kingdom of heaven, he didn't give them a sermon on humility, truthfulness, sincerity and simplicity. He just looked around, grabbed a child, and said, 'Here it is' (Matthew 18:2). That was teaching by parable.

A parable is a story or an action which conveys a truth in a vivid, concrete way. Matthew says that 'Jesus used parables to tell all these things to the crowds; he would not say a thing to them without using a parable.' (Matthew 13:34)

Read through Matthew chapter 13. It is a collection of seven parables which are designed to describe the nature of God's Kingdom. Most of them begin with 'The Kingdom of heaven is like this.'

Several points need to be made:
1   We may be too familiar with the stories to recognize how challenging they were to Jesus' audience. They weren't simple exhortations to be humble, loving or compassionate. They made unexpected demands and asked awkward questions.
2   We are handicapped by not being part of the original audience for which the parables were designed. The stories were set in a particular context which we may now know little about. Even Matthew heard the stories out of the original context.
3   The parables are open-ended. Of course they have a general purpose, but none of them has one precise meaning. Jesus' purpose was to make his hearers think for themselves and find their own meaning. He meant to shock them into a response.
4   The parable of the Sower and its 'explanation' (Matthew 13:1–23) presents a difficulty. According to Matthew (Mark is even harsher), Jesus used parables to make it impossible for some people to understand what he was saying. This is most unlikely. The strange text probably reflects a problem of the early church. How was it that Jesus' contemporaries failed to understand him? This text could be an attempt to offer an explanation.

'I will tell the harvest workers to pull up the weeds first'
Matthew 13:30

Jewish stories

The rabbi asked a rich man for a donation to help the hungry. The man refused saying the poverty was their own fault. The rabbi told him, 'Look out of the window. What do you see?' 'People', replied the rich man. 'Now look in your mirror. What do you see?' 'Myself, of course' said the man. 'Remarkable' said the rabbi. 'You only need to cover clear glass with a bit of silver, and you see only yourself.'

That's a Jewish parable.

Jesus didn't invent this way of teaching. He inherited it from his Jewish teachers, who always taught by telling stories. The Old Testament prophets were no exception. Here are a few examples.

> 1   Read Amos 7 : 7–9

Amos was a sheep farmer

Amos was a sheep farmer who became the first of the recorded prophets. He spoke out in a direct, uncompromising way against the corrupt life of the wealthy city-dwellers. He preached in the reign of Jeroboam II (783–743BC), a highly successful reign by material standards. But in order to produce the 'economic miracle' of that time the poor were being exploited. A self-satisfied Israel was worshipping a 'private' God—who was on their side. Amos saw his task as calling the people back to the Sinai Covenant. The God of Moses was the God who demanded justice for all people, especially the exploited.

In one of his sermons he uses a plumbline as a visual aid. God tests the wall (Israel) and finds it to be untrue. It *has* to be knocked down. God will destroy his people. The Assyrians invaded 30 years later.

Amos was probably addressing the crowd just as a builder in the background was using a plumbline. He might even have been addressing builders themselves!

> 2   Read Isaiah 5 : 1–7

Isaiah uses a striking way of preaching the same message. His parable is in the form of a poem. It is introduced as the kind of popular ballad that might be sung by minstrels at a feast, perhaps by Isaiah himself. He disguises his intention by keeping the punchline till the end. He sings of his friend's vineyard. It was tended so carefully that it promised a wonderful crop. But it produced bitter, wild grapes. It *had* to be destroyed. The vineyard, said Isaiah, was Israel. God had given so much to his people for no return. They would be ravaged. In fact, the Assyrians invaded soon afterwards.

3   *Read Jeremiah 18 : 1–12*

The prophets often used simple and familiar scenes for their parables. Here Jeremiah uses the imagery of a potter at his wheel. He acts out the parable. The message is the same as before. If the people of God are not true to the Covenant of Sinai, they must be broken like a misshapen pot on the potter's wheel. It needs to be remoulded.

Jesus' message, like theirs, was always a cry to Israel to be faithful to the Law of Moses (see part A). He used familiar scenes and images, as they did, to give colour to his stories.

Jesus used familiar scenes to give colour to his stories

List of Parables in Matthew's Gospel

There are about 50 parables in Matthew's Gospel, some quite short (Mark had only 17). Note that Matthew doesn't include the two best known parables, 'The Good Samaritan' and 'The Prodigal Son', which are found only in Luke.

The Kingdom of heaven is like:		Those unprepared for the Kingdom are like:	
City on a hill	5:14	Tasteless salt	5:13
Lamp on a lampstand	5:15	Lamp under a bowl	5:15
Riches kept safe	6:19	Debtor	5:25
Hungry son fed	7:9	Bad eyes	6:23
Narrow gate	7:13	Slave of two masters	6:24
House on rock	7:24	Unseen log	7:3
Doctor for the sick	9:12	Bad fruit tree	7:16
Bridegroom and guests	9:15		12:33
Victory over divided		House on sand	7:26
kingdom	12:25	Patched coat	9:16
Victory over strong		Old wineskins	9:17
man	12:29	Grumbling children	11:16
Abundant harvest	13:3	Empty house	12:43
Wheat and weeds	13:24	Blind leading the blind	15:14
Mustard tree	13:31	Bad weather	
Leavened bread	13:33	forecasters	16:2
Hidden treasure	13:44	Unforgiving servant	18:23
Precious pearl	13:45	Disgruntled workers	20:1
Netful of fish	13:47	Murderous vinedressers	21:33
New and old treasures	13:52	Man not dressed for a	
Lost sheep found	18:12	wedding	22:11
Father and two sons	21:28	Unfaithful servant	24:45
Wedding feast	22:1		
Many invited	22:14		
Vultures and carcase	24:28		
Flowering fig-tree	24:32		
One taken, one left	24:40		
Thief at night	24:42		
Bridegroom at night	25:1		
Money invested	25:14		

Palestine of the Gospels is now called Israel. It is a narrow strip of land between the Mediterranean Sea and the desert which lies east of the River Jordan.

It is a land of great contrasts:

1 The Jordan valley (part of the Great Rift Valley) lies below sea-level. It enjoys tropical climate and exotic vegetation along the river banks.

2 Northern Galilee is a mountainous, windy moorland, yet it descends to the hot shores of Lake Galilee.

3 The Plain of Esdraelon (Samaria of the Gospel) is warm and dry with extensive agriculture.

4 The Judaean hills in the South have a temperate climate. The land East of Jerusalem drops sharply to the Dead Sea—and the desert.

B8 Examples of parables in Matthew

Matthew has written his Gospel around five discourses, in which Jesus is presented as the great teacher (see page 64). The third of these discourses is chapter 13. It is addressed to the disciples and takes the form of a series of parables. Here we examine five parables, the last three of which don't appear in the other Gospels.

1 The hidden treasure

Read Matthew 13:44

A man finds hidden treasure in a field. He is overjoyed and sells up everything to buy the field. Hiding valuables in the ground (or in caves) was normal in Palestine during invasion. Treasure was sometimes unearthed years later.

2 The pearl

Read Matthew 13:45–46

A jeweller is on the search for the perfect pearl (then the most expensive of jewels). He is prepared to sell everything else he has to acquire it.

These parables are a pair, with the same general message: real treasure is worth enormous sacrifice. As so often in parallel stories, they balance by *contrast*. In the first the man is poor (he needs to sell *everything* just to buy a field). He comes across the treasure by chance.

In the second, the man is rich. He is searching for the perfect jewel.

The disciples are asked to make their conclusion. Jesus simply said 'The Kingdom of heaven is like this'. Did he mean that it is of immense value? Or that it remains hidden from most people? Or that it will cost enormous self-sacrifice to possess? Or that it will give great joy?

3 The net

Read Matthew 13:47–50

It is likely that the original parable was short, just v.47. 'The Kingdom of heaven is like this. Some fishermen throw their net out in the lake and catch all kinds of fish.' The dragnet in the parable was in common use as a way of fishing on Lake Galilee. The huge net picked up everything, good fish and bad. Was Jesus saying that saints and sinners are called to the Kingdom?

The story goes on to describe the sorting out of the fish, with some being rejected. For Matthew it became a parable of *Judgement*.

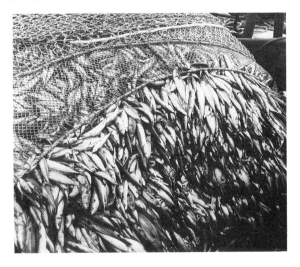

This is a good example of the way the early church allegorized the parables. An *allegory* is an interpretation of a story where each phrase, indeed each detail, is given a meaning. The Greeks tended to interpret stories this way. Jews did not. It is quite unlikely that the Jewish Jesus would have given a precise meaning to the end of his story; 'It will be like this at the end of the age' (v.49). This is probably Matthew's contribution. He was already deeply influenced by the Greek world into which the Church was expanding.

4   The unforgiving servant

Read Matthew 18:21–35

A king has a servant who has run up a staggering debt, millions of pounds. When he obviously can't pay it, the king commands him and his family to be sold into slavery. The servant begs for mercy. The king shows extraordinary compassion. He forgives him the debt and lets him go.

In utter contrast, the servant himself shows no compassion at all. A fellow servant owes him a hundred pounds. He demands repayment, refuses the plea for mercy, and throws the man into prison.

It is a story of contrasts. The two debts are fantastically different. The fellow servant could have repaid his debt over a few months. The first servant could *never* have repaid his debt. Yet the king shows un-conditional mercy. What are we to think of the servant's pitiless lack of mercy?

The story is a response to Peter's question about forgiveness. He thought he was being generous by suggesting forgiving his brother seven times. 'Not enough' said Jesus. 'Your forgiveness must be limitless, because that is how it is in God's Kingdom.' One commentator expressed the thrust of the story in these words:

> *Jesus took compassionate forgiveness as much for granted as the air he breathed. He did so because he knew this to be the atmosphere of the kingdom.*
>
> Edmund Flood

Matthew was sensitive to this particular teaching. The parable does not appear in the other evangelists. In Matthew it comes at the end of his fourth discourse, where Jesus is teaching his disciples how to live as a community. Compassion will be the measure of their faithfulness to God, who is a God of mercy rather than a God of justice. The parable is another way of saying: 'You must be perfect as your Father is perfect.' (See pages 15 and 26.)

Most commentators agree that the parable 'has nothing to do with punishment after death'. The final outcome of the incident (the king is angry with his servant's behaviour and punishes him)—is probably an addition. It bears the hallmark of Matthew's (and the early church's) interest in judgement. The last sentence, 'That is how my Father in heaven will treat each one of you unless you forgive your brother from your heart,' contradicts the original message of the parable. The words are presumably Matthew's, pointing a finger at unforgiving Christians.

5   The tenants in the vineyard

Read Matthew 21 : 33–46

This parable is recorded by all three synoptic writers. Some things never change. Wherever there are absentee landlords and poverty-stricken people, there is likely to be resentment, tension, even violence. This story tells of such a situation. Perhaps when Jesus told the story such an event was local news.

A landowner planted a vineyard and left it in the hands of tenants. He later sent agents to collect his share of the harvest. They were beaten, stoned and killed. More agents were sent and they were treated in the same way. So he finally sent his own son. He was thrown out of the vineyard and killed.

Based as it is on Isaiah's *Song of the Vineyard* (see page 46), the general purpose of this parable is clear. Like Isaiah, Jesus is issuing a warning to his people. They are the 'vineyard' on which God has lavished much loving care, with no return for his pains. If God's plans are now coming to a climax (the Kingdom is at hand), what ought God's people be doing?

Matthew has added many more details to this basic story than either Mark or Luke, turning it into a 'transparent allegory' (Wansbrough). Each detail of the story now has its own meaning:

• Mark's single agent twice becomes a whole group of agents. They represent the 'early' and 'later' prophets of Old Testament history. Matthew even has John the Baptist in mind. There is a reference to him eight verses earlier.

• One of the agents is stoned, as some of the prophets were.

• The son is killed *outside* the vineyard, not inside as in Mark. The reference is to Jesus' death outside the walls of Jerusalem.

• The landowner 'will certainly (literally "cruelly") kill those evil men' (v.41). The word 'cruel' refers to the terrible destruction of Jerusalem—which Matthew had witnessed, and Mark hadn't.

• The other tenants who took over the vineyard became 'a people' (v.43). For Matthew, the Gentile Church has taken over the role of Judaism. The Church is the new and true Israel.

Matthew has turned Jesus' parable into a direct confrontation with the Jewish authorities. The question with which it ends forces them unwittingly to condemn themselves. They seek to arrest him.

Questions and Things to Do

A   What do you know?

1   Why did Matthew speak of the Kingdom of *heaven*, rather than the Kingdom of God?

2   What is a parable?

3   Name three parables which begin 'The Kingdom of heaven is like . . .

4   What did Amos's image of a plumbline mean?

5   Outline Isaiah's parable of the vineyard.

6   About how many parables are recorded (a) by Mark (b) by Matthew?

7   Outline the parables of the Hidden Treasure and the Pearl.

8   What is an allegory?

9   What question did Peter ask that prompted Jesus to tell the parable of the Unforgiving Servant?

10   Name a parable which Matthew clearly turned into an allegory.

B   What do you understand?

1   How would you describe what Matthew meant by the Kingdom of heaven?

2   Why is it difficult for us to appreciate the original impact of the stories Jesus told?

3   In what way do the parables of The Hidden Treasure and The Pearl balance by contrast?

4   Why does it seem likely that Matthew added his own conclusion to Jesus' parable of The Net?

5   Outline the story of The Unforgiving Servant. Show how the ending is not in character with the spirit of the story.

C   What do you think?

1   Why do you think that the authorities were said to be angry when Jesus told the story of The Tenants in the Vineyard?

2   Write an essay with the title: 'Stories. A powerful way to teach.'

3   'Understanding and interpreting the parables isn't all that straightforward.' Comment.

D   Things to do

1   Prepare a slide programme which would illustrate the reading (with background music) of some of the shorter parables.

2   Make a collection of parables from other sources—including other religious traditions.

3   Make a large collage or frieze to illustrate the parables in Matthew.

4   Write a parable to accompany this photograph.

The Kingdom of heaven is like ......

> TASK
>
> Bring to the class/group a photo which you would entitle 'The Kingdom of heaven is like'

'When my house burnt down I got an unobstructed clear view of the moon.'
Zen saying

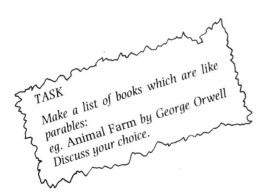

> TASK
> Make a list of books which are like parables:
> eg. Animal Farm by George Orwell
> Discuss your choice.

When the Wind Blows
'A visual parable against nuclear war ...'
The Sunday Times

B9　Jesus, who Acts in a prophetic manner

Take up thy bed and walk: An exultant Charpentier stands up for the first time in 19 years in the healing ceremony.

Lourdes works its miracle

ROBIN SMYTH ■ Paris

JOSEPH Charpentier's radiant face beams a belief in miracles as he walks a little gingerly, like a man with sore feet, round his village in the Moselle.

A few days ago Charpentier, 59, wheelchair-bound for 19 years, was among the throng of stretcher-case pilgrims praying for a cure at the Grotto at Lourdes in the Pyrenees.

'It happened during the healing ceremony in the basilica,' he says. 'Ten minutes after I had been anointed with holy oil I felt a great warmth rise from my feet to my heart.' He returned to his village pushing his wheelchair.

The villagers were amazed. But not everyone was convinced of a miracle. Charpentier's doctor was reserved. The former village priest, Father Didelon, said: 'I won't say it's a miracle but it's certainly extraordinary.'

Despite thousands of claims, the Catholic Church has officially proclaimed only 64 Lourdes miracles in the 130 years since a peasant girl, Bernadette, saw a vision of the Virgin there. Charpentier did not present his evidence to Lourdes' medical office.

A Paris physiotherapist commented: 'After 19 years in a wheelchair, leg muscles collapse entirely and can only be revived slowly. This recovery was too spectacularly quick to be plausible.'

A rheumatologist, Professor Martin-Francis Kahn, suggested that Charpentier might have been suffering from a psychic disorder in which the patient unconsciously simulates illness for his own advantage. The visit to Lourdes had produced a psychological shock which broke the syndrome.

Look carefully at the comments made by the doctor, the priest, the physiotherapist and the rheumatologist.

When is a miracle not a miracle?

310 The miracles of Jesus

Some years ago an American evangelist caused something of a sensation. Marjoe Gortner (the strange first name derives from the combination of Mary and Joseph), was trained from the age of ten to become an evangelist preacher and healer. He had an enthusiastic following and hundreds of cures to his credit when he suddenly withdrew from his ministry. He announced that he had never believed in God or in miracles, but only in his good training as a powerful preacher.

very age has its faith-healers. Some claim supernatural intervention. ome don't. Finbar Nolan of County Cavan, Ireland, doesn't consider the owers he has as 'miraculous'. But Harry Edwards, who successfully ealed people for years, claimed he had been helped by doctors and ealers who had passed over to the 'spirit world'.

If faith-healing is such a common phenomenon in human history, here does that leave the miraculous powers that Jesus seems to have ad? Don't Christians claim that he was 'something special'?

'Jesus went all over Galilee, teaching in the synagogues, preaching the ood News about the Kingdom, and *healing people who had all kinds of isease and sickness.*' (Matthew 4:23)

Before we look at some of the miracles in detail here are a few points to ear in mind.

It is clear that Jesus' public ministry was accompanied all the way through by miracles.

But then, miracles were common throughout Jewish history, especially within the prophetic movement.

Miracle stories also appear in all other religious traditions.

The early church took the miracles quite for granted. It is natural for a believer to see the miraculous wherever God's presence is felt. St Augustine of Hippo (died AD430) said that the multiplication of corn in a field is a miracle.

It was only people in later ages who spoke of the miracles as a knock-down *proof* that Jesus was approved by God. His deeds proved that his words were authentic.

By the 18th century a miracle was defined as 'an event or action which violates the laws of nature'. This emphasized the 'divinity' of Jesus. A Roman Catholic Council of bishops solemnly declared that miracles should be understood in this way. (Vatican I, 1870)

Today science no longer regards nature as bound by iron laws. Nor are many Christians happy with an image of Jesus as a kind of magician.

B11   The miracles in Matthew's Gospel

There are 18 miracle stories recorded in Matthew's Gospel. Yet alongside this miraculous element in Jesus' ministry there is a strong emphasis on 'playing down' the miracles. Matthew makes this point very clear at the beginning of the Gospel. Read again the temptations in the desert (Matthew 4:1–11). Jesus turns down the temptation to play the role of a wonderworker Messiah. The story 'stands as a parable of a whole lifetime of resistance to such a temptation'.

But Matthew recognized Jesus as the Messiah and carefully select‹ miracle stories (mainly from Mark) to show how he saw God at work Jesus. Matthew saw that Jesus by his words and deeds had brought abo‹ a *renewal* of creation. The stories can be put into three groups. It's helpf‹ to look at them in this way.

For Matthew, Jesus' miracles show him as bringing about:

The miracle of feeding a hungry world

1   *A healed world*

8:1	A leper (man with skin disease)
8:5	A paralytic boy (Roman officer's servan‹
8:14	Peter's mother-in-law
9:2	A paralyzed man
9:20	A woman with severe bleeding
9:27	Two blind men*
20:29	
12:10	Man with paralyzed hand

2   *A sinless world*

8:28	Gadarene demons
9:32	A dumb demoniac
12:22	A blind and dumb demoniac*
15:21	A demoniac girl
17:14	A demoniac boy

3   *A transformed world*

8:23	A storm is stilled
9:18	The dead are restored to life
14:13	The hungry are fed (5000)
15:32	The hungry are fed (4000)
14:23	The waves are conquered

There are also several references to an unspecified number who w‹ sick or possessed by demons.

Note   Miracles related only in Matthew are marked with an asterisk*

1   A Healed World

The stories in this first group describe Jesus' healing of physically s‹ people. Matthew has eight examples, the first being the healing of a lep‹

Jesus heals a leper

Read Matthew 8 : 1–4

Lepers were outcasts. They had to give warnings of their arrival so that everyone could get out of the way. Anyone touching a leper shared his uncleanness.

This scene tells us a great deal about Jesus. (Mark tells the story in more detail and expresses the emotional response of Jesus.) Matthew reduces the incident to an outline. Notice the following details:

- The man senses he does not have to keep away from Jesus.
- He has faith in Jesus' power to cure.
- Jesus deliberately 'touches him', thereby making himself unclean in the eyes of the Law.
- Jesus doesn't want his act of compassion made public.
- He asks the man to follow the requirements of the Law (see Leviticus 14 : 1–32), so that he can return to social life.

The story tells us that Jesus remains faithful to Jewish Law. But if human compassion is in conflict with the Law, Jesus has no hesitation in putting compassion first. He touches the untouchable man. The story is placed immediately after the teaching on the mountain, which finished with the words:

> *He wasn't like the teachers of the Law; instead he taught with authority.*
> Matthew 7 : 29

Matthew places a number of miracle stories at this point. He sees the actions of Jesus as conferring on him an authority that cannot be questioned.

In curing this skin disease, Jesus acts in the tradition of the prophet Elisha.

Naaman is cured

Read 2 Kings 5 : 1–27

Elisha was the disciple of the great prophet Elijah, in 9th-century Israel. In this story he cures the Syrian commander Naaman of a dreaded skin disease, probably a mild form of leprosy (Naaman was not an outcast). Naaman then confesses faith in the God of Israel. Notice the following details:

- The touching faith of the servant girl moves Naaman to a similar faith.
- Naaman is sent to wash in the Jordan, scene of Jesus' baptism.
- Naaman professes faith in Israel's God, Yahweh.
- Naaman is a Gentile. Luke, the evangelist of the Gentiles, makes much of this detail:

> *There were many suffering from a dreaded skin-disease who lived in Israel during the time of the prophet Elisha; yet not one of them was healed, but only Naaman the Syrian.* Luke 4 : 27

Jesus heals a Roman officer's servant

> Read Matthew 8 : 5–13

In the story of the healing of the skin disease, Matthew established that Jesus was faithful to the Jewish Law. In this next scene, he shows Jesus praising the Gentiles at the expense of the Jews. When Matthew wrote his Gospel the church was largely a Gentile one. Jesus' own ministry had been confined almost entirely to Jews, but Matthew found in the Q source this miracle story which prepared the way for the Gentile expansion. Notice the details of the story:

1   Matthew's story is simpler than Luke's. The Roman officer speaks face to face with Jesus.
2   He shows absolute faith in the power of Jesus to heal.
3   He says he doesn't deserve Jesus' presence in the home. So Jesus heals at a distance.
4   Matthew says that Jesus was surprised to find such faith *outside* of Israel. Does this suggest a Jesus who is prejudiced?
5   Matthew here adds verses 11–12.

> *I assure you that many will come from the east and the west and sit down with Abraham, Isaac, and Jacob at the feast in the Kingdom of heaven. But those who should be in the Kingdom will be thrown out into the darkness, where they will cry and grind their teeth.*

(Matthew liked this latter phrase. See 13:42, 50; 22:13; 24:51 and 25:30.)

One commentator remarks: 'Matthew must have written verses 10–12 with a deep sadness in his heart.' (Michael Fallon)

It was an admission that many of his own people had less faith and humility than some of the Gentiles. And faith and humility are the passports to the Kingdom.

A sandal found at Masada

Roman occupation

At the time of Jesus Palestine was under Roman rule as part of the Roman province of Syria. Earlier it had been ruled by Herod the Great as Rome's appointed 'king'. At his death in 4BC, Rome allowed the kingdom to be divided between his three sons, Herod Antipas, Philip and Archelaus. Archelaus' rule of Judaea was a cruel one. He was eventually deposed by Rome in AD6 and replaced by 'direct rule' in the person of a Governor.

Roman soldiers were therefore a familiar sight in Palestine. The main garrison was at Caesarea-on-Sea, but there was a detachment in Jerusalem at Herod the Great's Antonia fortress. This overlooked the Temple area, a potential trouble spot in the city.

Visitors to Israel today go to *Masada* on the Dead Sea where the Romans took over Herod's palace as a garrison. In AD66, patriotic Jews known as Zealots captured it. Their 'sit-in' lasted five years. They finally committed mass suicide rather than surrender to the Roman army.

Jesus heals a paralyzed man

> *Read Matthew 9:1–7*

Some people brought a paralyzed man, still on his bed, to Jesus. The healing forms a climax to the earlier healing stories. Jesus not only heals a man of his sickness, he proclaims that his sins are forgiven. The points to notice in this story are:

1 The teachers of the Law are challenged. Jesus seems to provoke them deliberately by claiming a power which belongs to God alone— forgiving sins.
2 The man's friends have faith in Jesus. (Matthew trims Mark's account and doesn't convey the extraordinary persistence they showed in getting the man to Jesus). The evangelists are emphasizing the importance of community faith.
3 Jesus responds to the popular belief that sickness is the result of sin. When the man is cured, it is a sign that his sin has been forgiven.
4 The story suggests that the teachers of the Law are evaluating Jesus. In reality, says Matthew, Jesus is the only one in a position to judge others.
5 Matthew changes Mark's ending to the story. 'The people...were afraid, and praised God for giving such *authority to men*.' The crowd only saw one man, Jesus, with the authority to forgive sin. Matthew is thinking of the disciples' share in the power to forgive sins.

What do these stories mean?

Many people ask what really happened? They would like an actual eye-witness report of events. If photographs were available, all the better. But the emphasis in these healing stories is not on what actually happened, but on the effect they had on the disciples. 'A miracle can be defined as an event which produces *wonder* and acts as a *sign* of the presence and *action* of God.' (Fallon) (The New Testament uses three Greek words for miracles, *teras* = wonder; *semeion* = sign; and *dynamis* = power.)

Scholars today conclude:

• Jesus performed marvels. And he said his disciples could do even better.
• The early disciples never asked 'Did this happen?' They asked 'What does it mean?'
• Some of the miracle cures may be explicable in terms of psychosomatic illness (the mind and body affect each other). Love and compassion can heal.
• The ultimate miracle, the New Testament claims, was Jesus himself— his extraordinary ability to communicate God's healing love.

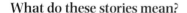

2   A Sinless World

Jesus heals a demoniac girl

> *Read Matthew 15:21–28*

Matthew tells five stories of Jesus casting out *demons*. In New Testament times mental illness (manic depression, psychiatric disorders, etc) was thought to be the presence of evil spirits living in people. People were afraid of the demons, although they didn't regard demon-possession as a punishment for sin. It was sheer misfortune. The demons were a fact of life, the evidence of a power of evil existing alongside the good.

Matthew sees the Jesus who casts out these demons as replacing the Rule of Satan with the Rule of God. The Kingdom of heaven is at hand.

The importance of this miracle story:

1   Jesus' power is greater than that of the demons.
2   The scene follows yet another confrontation with the Jewish authorities. Are they too possessed by demons? By contrast the Canaanite woman—a Gentile—recognizes Jesus when they had failed to do so. It is she who has great *faith*.
3   Jesus' mission is restricted to his own Jewish people. Here he refers to non-Jews contemptuously as 'dogs'. Prejudice or tongue-in-cheek? It would seem that Jesus himself made no overtures to the non-Jewish world. That was left to the disciples later. (See also page 58, Matthew 8:5–13, where Jesus doesn't go to the Roman officer's home; in both miracle stories he heals from a distance.)

What does this story mean?

It is likely that the girl suffered a mental disorder. Jesus' love and compassion reached out to her. His was a healing love, replacing the fear which others showed for her. It does not make a miracle any less of a marvel if it can be explained in human terms. It is in and through the human experience that God always works.

Even today some people FEAR those who are mentally sick. The constant loving care shown for this autistic boy is a miracle of compassion. Do you agree?

3   A Transformed World

The five miracle stories in this group are often known as 'nature' miracles.

A storm is stilled

Read Matthew 8 : 23–27

It is no longer possible to know precisely what gave rise to this story. But it is possible to discover what such a story meant to Matthew and the early church.

In one way the story is like an exorcism. Jesus commands the winds and waves in the same way as he commands devils. The sea was thought of as a powerful demon threatening to overwhelm Israel. Only God could overcome such an evil. No wonder the disciples were left awestruck.

The following points help us to understand Matthew's further thinking:
• The story follows Jesus' response to two candidates for discipleship. To follow Jesus is to follow into a hostile environment.
• Matthew emphasizes Jesus' power to protect those who become his disciples.
• Matthew's disciples show more faith than Mark's.
'Teacher, don't you care for us?' (Mark)
'Save us, Lord.' (Matthew)
• Matthew would also have had in mind the Old Testament story of Moses commanding the sea before his frightened people. Jesus is a new Moses.

Crossing the Sea

Read Exodus 14 : 5–31

Israel, the nation, was born when it escaped from Egypt in the 13th century BC. This crossing of the sea marked its passing over from slavery into freedom. The story, told and retold, has become an epic, where it is no longer possible to tell precisely what originally happened. What is clear is that Israel saw God's hand in every event, even a natural one. Here he is said to raise the wind deliberately to protect his people. Later writers have added the detail of Moses parting the sea with his staff—to emphasize his leadership.

Matthew tells another 'nature' miracle about the sea to emphasize the power of God in Jesus, and to point to the role of Peter.

The waves are conquered

Read Matthew 14 : 22–33

Mark had told a story of Jesus walking over the water to rescue his frightened friends. Matthew adds a detail of Peter trying to walk out to meet him. It is the first of three *Peter incidents* (see 16 : 16–20, 17 : 24–27). All three emphasize the leadership of Peter in the church.

Some commentators wonder if this is a misplaced resurrection story. It finishes with the disciples' *worship* of Jesus: 'Truly you are the Son of God.' The full understanding of this could only come after the Resurrection.

The hungry are fed

> *Read Matthew 14:13–21*

The story of walking on the water was preceded by a story in which a crowd of thousands of people are miraculously fed. This story is almost repeated in Matthew 15:32–39. Both miracles are discussed in an incident recorded in chapter 16.

These three chapters (14–16) form a series of instructions to the disciples, which lead to Peter's profession of faith in 16:16.

Thus: Matthew 14:13   Feeding of five thousand (bread)
                15:32   Feeding of four thousand (bread)
                16:7   Discussion about bread
                16:16   Peter's profession.

Why does Matthew tell the feeding story twice? Some commentators see this as an echo of the Old Testament stories in which God feeds his people over and over again in the desert (see below).

Others point to the different number of baskets in the two stories and suggest that Matthew wants to show that both Jews (12 tribes) and Gentiles (7 nations, see Acts 13:19) are offered salvation.

Different commentators have different views on the sort of event which could have given rise to these feeding stories.

1 The text describes accurately what actually happened. Jesus literally multiplied one picnic lunch into enough food to feed thousands.
2 The bread was not miraculous but providential: Jesus knew a secret store of food in a cave, and helped himself.
3 The story is an exaggeration of an event which really involved only a few hundred people.
4 The story is a parable about the joy people find in sharing.
5 The story is about the power of Jesus' preaching, which was so hypnotic that people felt satisfied with only a few crumbs each.
6 The story is purely symbolic. Jesus is presented as greater than Elisha who fed a crowd with only 20 loaves (see 2 Kings 4:42–44). Indeed, he is the awaited Messiah, whose coming is often spoken of in the Old Testament in terms of a banquet. Matthew would have the last Supper and its enactment in mind.

The setting for the story is 'a lonely place', or desert. Matthew has Moses in mind.

The Manna in the desert

> *Read Exodus 16:1–36*

When the Israelites were in the desert they fed on 'manna', a honeylike substance formed in springtime by insects living on tamarisk trees. (It still exists in the Sinai desert.) The strict regulations about collecting the manna came from Old Testament tradition, where Sabbath regulations were important.

Some Jews expected that when the Messiah came the wonders of the exodus would be renewed as signs of God's providence and presence.

The dead are restored to life

Read Matthew 9:18–19, 23–26

I DIED IN CHILDBIRTH

When I look at my daughter I know what a miracle it is that we are both still here. Not many people die and then get given a second chance . . .

This mother is one of many people who have medically died during childbirth and come back to life. She knows that miracles happen. Her daughter will always remind her of that.

Matthew records a miracle story which in a few words records the anguish-turned-to-joy of another family. An official (called Jairus by Mark) comes to Jesus saying his daughter has died. He simply and reverently believes that Jesus can bring her back to life. Jesus goes to the home, sends the mourners and traditional wailers away, and takes the little girl by the hand. She recovers. The story is well publicized. Such a miracle of death-to-life is bound to make people sit up and take notice.

What really happened? Did the young child die in the way the mother above had 'died'? Or was she medically dead for a long time, making her recovery *quite beyond* what is humanly possible? We can never answer these questions. But it is clear what Matthew had in mind:
1. In Jesus the power of God is shown to be stronger than death.
2. Jesus responds to the faith of the girl's father.
3. Jesus is always ready to help to bring joy where there is anguish.
4. Matthew has again rearranged Mark to draw attention to the disciples. (Compare Mark 5:24 and Matthew 9:19.) For Matthew, the disciples both witness the miracle and themselves inherit the power of God. (See page 64.)

It is also likely that Matthew had in mind a similar story attributed to the prophet Elisha.

Elisha restores a child's life

Read 2 Kings 4:18–37

The woman from Shunem has a son only after Elisha has prayed for her. The boy is taken ill and dies. His mother has absolute faith in Elisha. She rushes to him and stays at his side, even when the servant Gehazi goes on ahead to hold Elisha's staff (remember the staff of Moses) over the boy. The stick cannot work a miracle, it needs the power and presence of the prophet, God's spokesman. Matthew was very sensitive to this. The presence of Jesus was always life-giving.

This happy, healthy boy is a miracle to his adoptive parents. Doctors don't understand how he recovered from the point of death. When discovered in a Colombian shanty town he weighed 4 lbs. He was 7 months old.

B12 Conclusion

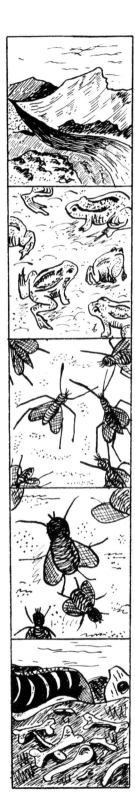

Plan of Matthew's Gospel		
Introduction	Infancy	ch 1–2
Book 1	Narrative	ch 3–4
	Discourse	ch 5–7
Book 2	Narrative	ch 8–9
	Discourse	ch 10
Book 3	Narrative	ch 11–12
	Discourse	ch 13:2–13:52
Book 4	Narrative	ch 13:53–17:27
	Discourse	ch 18
Book 5	Narrative	ch 19–23
	Discourse	ch 24–25
Conclusion	Passion Narrative	ch 26–28

Matthew set out his Gospel very carefully. It is arranged as five books, with an introduction and a conclusion. Each book consists of a discourse preceded by a narrative. The miracle stories are very carefully placed in the text. They appear in two of the five books.

1   In the second book (chapters 8–10)

This book shows Jesus to be the new Moses by his actions. The narrative in chapters 8 and 9 consists of ten miracle stories. They echo Moses' ten plagues. (Exodus 7:14–9:35) Jesus' miracles are *signs* that the Messianic era had arrived. The ten stories lead into a missionary discourse. Jesus begins his instruction to the Apostles by sending them out to work miracles themselves (Matthew 10:1, 8).

2   In the fourth book (Matthew 13:53–18:35)

In the discourse of chapter 18 Jesus tells the disciples how the new Messianic community (the Church) should live. The central message is loving care for all, especially the weak. The narrative which introduces this discourse includes miracles which are signs of compassion and love.

Such careful and artificial planning leads many commentators to conclude that the miracle stories are not necessarily straightforward historical reports of unnatural happenings. Some Christians are unhappy about this, suspecting that scholars 'explain the miracle away'. They want miracles to be miracles. If all sense of wonder is lost, what happens to the uniqueness of Jesus?

Other Christians accept that the historical facts are lost. The question 'What really happened?' can't be answered. But one question can be answered: 'What did miracles mean to Matthew?'

Matthew used miracle stories to illustrate his conviction that Jesus was from God. He was the expected Messiah, the fulfilment of all Old Testament hopes, the salvation of the Jews and of all people. With his coming the Kingdom of God had arrived. Miracles were the sign that this was so.

B13 Summary

Prophets forth-tell—they come out boldly with the truth. This is usually a most unpopular thing to do, and prophets can find their lives very uncomfortable. Nelson Mandela has been imprisoned for over 25 years for his outspoken call for equality amongst black and white people in South Africa.

Amongst all the Old Testament prophets, Jeremiah stands out for his unwavering loyalty to God in the face of terrible hostility. His life was a martyrdom. He was put in stocks, imprisoned, tried for blasphemy, flogged and dropped into a well to starve. He was later released but eventually forced into exile in Egypt. A late Jewish legend says he died there, stoned by fellow Jews.

Read the incident of the well.

> *Jeremiah 38:1–13*

It is only Matthew who sees Jesus as a Jeremiah figure. In the important scene where Peter professes his faith in Jesus, only Matthew includes Jeremiah in the dialogue. Compare Matthew 16:14, Mark 8:28, Luke 9:19. Matthew saw Jesus as *the* prophet who spoke forth the truth. This made him so unpopular that it led to his death. He describes the beginning of this movement towards a final confrontation by telling of Jesus' 'messianic entry' into Jerusalem.

> *Read Matthew 21:1–17*

Matthew sees Jesus' entry into Jerusalem as the fulfilment of a number of Old Testament texts. It is likely that Jesus and his disciples arrived in Jerusalem quite simply alongside other pilgrims. There they would have been greeted with palm branches and acclamations from Psalm 118, regular features of the Jewish feast of Tabernacles and Dedication of the Temple (see Psalm 118:27).

But for Matthew this is something more, and he has carefully chosen Old Testament texts to say so:

1 He sees it as symbolic (so did Mark) that Jesus arrives on a donkey. *Zechariah* 9:9 had described a peaceful messianic figure in these terms.
2 The same book of Zechariah promised that 'when that time comes, there will no longer be any merchant in the Temple of the Lord Almighty' (14:21). For Matthew, Jesus' action fulfils this promise.
3 Matthew alone refers to Jesus in this scene as 'the prophet'. (Matthew 21:10–11) He therefore denounces wrong in the way prophets always did.
4 Jesus goes to the Temple *immediately* to purify it (Mark leaves it till the next day). He is fulfilling *Malachi*'s promise that 'the Lord you are looking for will suddenly come to his Temple . . . He will be . . . like a fire that refines metal . . . He will purify the priests'. (Malachi 3:2–3)

Questions and Things to Do

A What do you know?

1 About how many miracle stories are recorded in Matthew?

2 When did people begin to think of a miracle as 'an event which violates the laws of nature'?

3 Miracle stories are sometimes put into 3 groups. What are they? Describe each.

4 Name a miracle story in which Jesus does not want it made public.

5 Who told Naaman about the prophet Elijah?

6 To whom did Jesus say: 'Courage, my son! Your sins are forgiven'?

7 What do the Greek words *teras, semeion* and *dynamis* mean?

8 Name two miracle stories in which Jesus responds to Gentiles.

9 How did the Jewish people regard the sea?

10 How were the people fed in the desert at the time of the exodus?

B What do you understand?

1 What evidence is there that Jesus played down his ability to work miracles?

2 Describe two miracle stories that emphasize the need for *faith*.

3 Quote two texts that suggest Jesus addressed himself to his fellow Jews, and not to the Gentiles.

4 Outline the story of the exodus and show how Matthew possibly had it in mind when recording at least two miracle stories.

5 'Prophets don't foretell the future; they call people to live just, honest, faithful lives.' Comment, with reference to at least two prophets.

C What do you think?

1 'I want a miracle to be a miracle.' What do you understand by this statement?

2 Give a short outline of the life of Jeremiah. Do you think all prophets are likely to suffer as he did? Give reasons for your answer.

3 Do miracles still happen?

4 Write a newspaper report under the headline: 'Nazareth wonder-worker comes to town.'

D Things to do

1 Make a frieze depicting the miracle stories recorded by Matthew.

2 Write a song describing either a miracle of Jesus or miracles you see in daily life. (Could you include both?)

3 Find a picture or newspaper cutting to illustrate your view of miracles.

4 An Argus poster reads 'Miracles happen only to those who believe in them.' Choose a picture which could be used for this poster.

5 Make a collage entitled 'Today's Prophets'.

'The impossible we do immediately.
Miracles take a little longer.'
General Alexander 1945

TASK

Organize your group to do the exercise below. Display and discuss the results.

A fifth year group were asked to give an example of what they would call a miracle. They had to bring to class a photo or cutting to illustrate their answer. Here are 4 of their examples.

1   'Visions are miracles. It is usually Mary who appears, like at Medjugorje.'

Virgin gives Paris an oily miracle

From Patrick Marnham
in Paris

A MIRACLE is said to have been observed in the fashionable 16th *arrondissement* of Paris. Bassam Assaf, a devout member of the Greek Orthodox Church, reports that in the past six months, while praying in a private chapel, he has experienced five apparitions of the Virgin Mary.

On 12 August, when the second apparition occurred, he was praying before a statue of the Virgin when oil began to flow from his hands. Since then hundreds of witnesses have observed the oil, and stories of miraculous cures have begun to circulate.

Nazir Fansa, 69, a Sunni Mus-

AFP, sent reporters and photographers to the chapel, where they interviewed Mr Assaf and photographed the phenomenon.

Mr Assaf works as a se⸍ for a Syrian business⸍ the chapel is in his h⸍ the Holy Virgin dr⸍ with a white, bl⸍ Mr Assaf sa⸍ protect ⸍ hand⸍ r⸍

2   'I think it's a miracle when people like the former BA stewardess, Maura McDonagh, work for the third World.'

3   'This view, out of my bedroom window, at 7.00 am.'

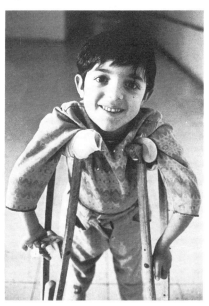

4   'When handicapped people smile and get on with life. I couldn't.'

Extended Question

'A man has no share in the Torah, unless he believes that all things and all events in the life of the individual as well as in the life of society are miracles. There is no such thing as the natural course of events.' Nachmanides

At 5½ years old life is beautifully simple.

Any time you're thirsty, day or night, a cool refreshing glass of sparkling clean water is always there on tap.

Taken for granted by Katy (and by most of our other fifty million customers) that small miracle is brought about daily by the Water Authorities of England and Wales.

The specialist skills of some 50,000 people see to it that the quality of the 130 litres of water which we each use every day is every bit as good as Katy's night-time tipple.

And that the water that's used is treated before it's returned to our lakes, rivers and the sea.

In the care that we take to look after water and our customers, we've developed a friendly working relationship with a great many people as well as Mother Nature.

Hence the theme of this year's Observer National Children's Poetry Competition: Friendship.

(You'll find details of the competition, sponsored by the Water Authorities, in this magazine.)

And if you'd like to know more about what we do, we'd be happy to tell you. Just fill in the coupon above.

A small miracle, twenty-four hours a day.

1 What is the small miracle in the advert? (1)
2 Why would it be a 'great' miracle if the girl lived in Bangladesh? (1)
3 Describe a Gospel story about a young girl and a miracle. (4)
4 Gospel miracle stories can be divided into three groups. (6)
(a) How are they divided? (b) Give an example for each group.

5 Do you agree with Nachmanides that 'All events in life are miracles'? Explain your answer. (4)
6 Design an advert which promotes a 'miracle . . . . .' (4)

Useful Addresses

Church Missionary Society Ireland
12 Talbot Street, Belfast BT1 2LE

Belfast Bible College
Glenburn House, Glenburn Road South, Dunmurry, Belfast BT17 9JP

Volunteer Missionary Movement (RC)
13 Herma Street, Glasgow G23 5AW and High Park, Grace Park Road, Dublin 9

Society of Jesus (RC)
114 Mount Street, London W1Y 6AH

Useful Reading

Martin Luther King *Strength To Love* Fontana 1969
Eknath Easwaran *Gandhi The Man* Turnstone Press, Wellingborough, Northants
Malcolm Muggeridge *Something Beautiful for God* (Mother Teresa of Calcutta) Fontana 1972
Bishop Desmond Tutu *Hope and Suffering* Fount 1983
Bob Geldof *Is That It?* Penguin 1986

Part C

The Promised Deliverer

C1   Infancy stories

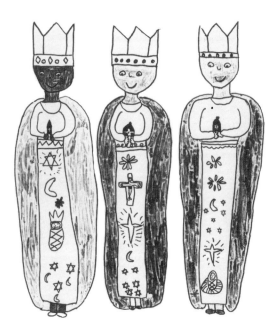

One of the most familiar stories about Jesus is the Christmas story. Collect together some Christmas cards and display them. Look up the four Gospels and find out which parts of the traditional Gospel story are portrayed on the cards. And go through your repertoire of carols to do the same.

You will discover that Matthew and Luke are the only two Gospels to mention Jesus' birth and youth. You'll also notice that the stories they tell are quite different. This is the first *clue* that you may not be reading a straightforward historical account of what happened two thousand years ago.

How did the Christmas stories come about?

The earliest preaching about Jesus (the 'kerygma', see page 2) concentrated on his public, adult life. The Christmas stories were the last additions to the Gospel.

The stories in the Gospels are sometimes about public, observable incidents, and sometimes about private, hidden experiences of Jesus (eg. temptation in the desert, agony in the garden . . .). The infancy stories belong to this second type. They are therefore theological rather than factual stories. They convey a deep truth about Jesus. The stories tell us what the writers understand Jesus to be. This does *not* make them trivial stories. On the contrary, it makes them important reflections on the identity of Jesus. For this reason the churches have always celebrated Christmas with great solemnity and joy.

The Christmas Festival

Christmas is now celebrated in Western Christian communities on December 25th. This was the day on which pagan Rome celebrated mid-winter, and welcomed the New Birth of the Sun as days began to grow longer. Christians 'baptized' this feast, to welcome Christ as the Light of the World. The Sun became the Son.

The older feast of Christmas was kept on January 6th. It was known as the Manifestation of God, and celebrated the birth of Jesus, the adoration of the Magi (see page 75), and the baptism in which Jesus was proclaimed Son of God. Eastern Orthodox Christians still keep Christmas on that day.

C2 Matthew's Christmas Story

Matthew, the most Jewish of the evangelists, tells the story of Jesus in a way with which Jews were familiar. He tells stories to show the meaning of the events, not to record biographical detail. His readers would immediately detect parallels in the Old Testament and in Jewish tradition. Occasionally he quotes from Scriptures to make his point very clear.

Matthew's purpose was to show that Jesus was the Messiah. This belief of his was based on his experience of Jesus' resurrection. But if Jesus was the Messiah, then all that the prophets had said was fulfilled in him even at his birth.

The first two chapters of the Gospel are written around five Old Testament quotations, each introduced by the rubric, 'This happened to make what the Lord had said through the prophet come true.' All the quotations refer to events that had already taken place in the past. But Matthew maintains that the hopes expressed in these texts were only completely fulfilled when Jesus came on the scene.

The five quotations referred to are as follow:

1   Virgin birth   Matthew 1:22
2   Bethlehem   2:5
3   Flight into Egypt   2:15
4   Slaughter of the innocents   2:17
5   Nazareth   2:23

In addition to these explicit quotations Matthew makes passing allusions to many other Old Testament themes. After carefully analyzing the text, scholars have come to the conclusion that Matthew saw all the themes of the Old Testament come together in Jesus as Messiah, not because that was predicted by individual prophets, but because he was the new Passover, the new liberator of Israel, the new King of the Jews.

One commentator has expressed it like this:

It is in Jesus' death and resurrection that Matthew discovered Jesus to be the new Moses rescuing his people from slavery, the new David bringing about the kingdom of God on earth, the new Solomon in all his glory, the new Israel rising out of the ashes of the old. It was the facts of Jesus' life and death, not of his birth, which justified such a theology.

       The First Christmas What Really Happened?   H J Richards

1   The New Moses

We already know that Matthew saw Jesus as the new Moses, the saviour of his people. Over the years the rabbis had elaborated the Bible story of Moses:

Moses' birth was foretold to his father in a dream,
Pharaoh was warned beforehand of the birth,
Pharaoh consulted his astrologers to know what to do.

Moses led his people into the desert

Read Matthew chapters 1 and 2

It is not difficult to see that Matthew had these Moses stories in mind. Pharaoh tried to get rid of the baby Moses. Herod tried to get rid of the baby Jesus. Later Moses led his people away from the slavery of Egypt. As if to come full circle, Jesus was led back to the safety of Egypt. The time would come when Jesus would found a new people, and lead them to the new Kingdom.

2   The New David

After the exodus, and Moses' death, the people settled in the land of Canaan. Eventually under David they became a kingdom. All Jews looked back to the time of King David as the ideal period of their history. They longed for a second David. The promised Messiah was seen as a descendant of David, God's own representative who finally established peace on earth.

Matthew left his readers in no doubt that he saw Jesus as the second David.

Genealogy

Read Matthew 1:1–17

The Gospel begins 'This is the list of the ancestors [genesis] of Jesus Christ, a descendant of David, who was a descendant of Abraham.' Jesus was therefore, thoroughly Jewish. Verse 17 says: 'So then, there were fourteen generations from Abraham to David, and fourteen from David to the exile in Babylon, and fourteen from then to the birth of the Messiah.' Each Hebrew letter had a number equivalent. The sum of the letters for *David* is fourteen. Numbers were significant to the Jews. *Seven* is the perfect number. As Matthew had 3×14 or 6×7, it meant that Jesus was the beginning of the seventh seven. This is perfection.

The birth story

Read Matthew 1:18–24

Matthew's story is rich in explicit and implicit references to the Old Testament.

Dreams

Joseph is more prominent in Matthew's birth story than in Luke's. In good Old Testament style he is told of the special nature of Jesus' birth in a dream. The angel tells him that he has a place in this dream. The text doesn't suggest that Joseph suspected Mary of adultery. He knows she is special to God and offers to step back. His role, as son of David, is to place Jesus in the line of David.

Isaiah

The quotation 'a virgin will become pregnant and have a son, and he will be called Immanuel (which means "God is with us")' would send Matthew's readers to Isaiah 7:14. They would understand it in context. Isaiah wrote when Israel was in political crisis. He promised the 'Virgin Israel' that God would send a royal son if she relied on God, not on military power. The son was born, Hezekiah, whom history recognized as one of the greatest of David's descendants. It was said of him: 'He was faithful to the Lord and never disobeyed him, but carefully kept all the commandments that the Lord had given Moses. So the Lord was with him.' (2 Kings 18:6–7). Matthew says that the child born of the Virgin Mary is an even greater example of God being with his people.

Micah

To emphasize the royal dynasty Matthew places Jesus' birth in Bethlehem where David was born. (Matthew 2:5–8) He quotes from Micah, a contemporary of Isaiah, who was assuring the people that Israel would prevail over its enemies. David's dynasty would last.

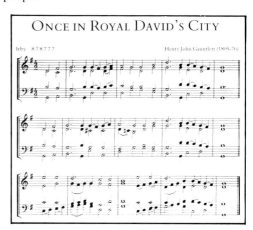

ONCE IN ROYAL DAVID'S CITY

Irby 878777   Henry John Gauntlett (1805–76)

Implicit references

Matthew had no doubt that Jesus was heir to the promises made to David. His readers would quite naturally turn to Old Testament texts, even ones that Matthew does not quote. This, for example, is how the prophet Nathan passed on God's message to David:

> *When you die and are buried with your ancestors, I will make one of your sons king and will keep his kingdom strong. He will be the one to build a temple for me, and I will make sure that his dynasty continues for ever. I will be his father, and he will be my son.* 2 Samuel 7:12–14

The Virgin Birth

Some Christians find it very important to believe that Mary was literally always a virgin. Their faith is in a God who can do the impossible.

Other Christians can't believe in a God who intervenes in history to alter the rules. They find it important to believe that Mary was not literally a virgin. Is there any evidence to support this view?

Of the New Testament writers, only Matthew and Luke speak of Jesus being born of 'a virgin'. Matthew underlines the theme by saying that Jesus fulfils the text of Isaiah 7, 'A virgin will become pregnant and have a son.'

Those who understand this as a supernatural prodigy—making Jesus quite unlike any other human being—are missing the Old Testament overtones of such language.

The Old Testament is full of stories of children born 'of God'. For the believer every child is a gift of God, but especially if he or she becomes a leader of God's people.

Such children are not simply the result of human effort: they are *Godsends*. If that is true of so many Old Testament heroes, what else can a Christian say about Jesus except that he comes *totally* from God? His mother Mary is shown alongside Tamar, Rahab, Ruth and Uriah's wife (Ancestry, Matthew 1:2–8). These four women were most unlikely candidates for God's blessings. Matthew saw Mary as part of this pattern. She was the supreme example of the emptiness of the human race filled to overflowing by a God who is sheer grace.

Does the text tell us whether, over and above this theme of human emptiness, Mary was literally and biologically a virgin? No. Matthew shows no interest in such a modern question. He does not hesitate to put his story of 'virgin birth' next to a genealogy which specifies Jesus as a descendant of Joseph.

All Christians, but in particular Roman Catholics, whatever their interpretation of the Virgin Birth, have the deepest reverence for Mary as the mother of the man whom they acknowledge as the Son of God. Across the ages theologians, artists and poets have expressed this eloquently.

3   The New Solomon

Poets have often written about the story of the 'Three Kings'. Artists have drawn it and children acted it out in nativity plays. So it is a shock to some people to discover that, in Matthew's text, the Magi are neither three nor kings. He speaks of 'some men who studied the stars'. (Matthew 2:1)

> Read Matthew 2:1–12

This colourful story is another meditation by Matthew on Old Testament themes which he applies to Jesus. This Jewish form of writing is called *midrash*. Notice:

1   Matthew will later speak of Jesus as 'greater than Solomon' (12:42). Here he anticipates that theme by reminding readers of the Queen of Sheba's visit to Solomon, bringing gifts of gold, spices and jewels (read 1 Kings 10:1–13). Jesus is the new Solomon.
2   The exit cue is the same in both stories.
    'Then she ... returned to the land of Sheba.' (1 Kings 10:13)
    'Then they returned to their country.' (Matthew 2:12)
3   Ancient literature often speaks of the birth of great people in terms of a new star in the sky. A rabbinic story tells of the Queen of Sheba being guided to Solomon by a star. There is no need to study astrology to understand Matthew's story.
4   Matthew probably sees the Magi as representing the whole Gentile world coming to accept this new Solomon. While everyone in Jerusalem is upset (v.3), they are full of joy (v.11).

4   The New Israel

The Old Testament prophets looked forward to the descendant of David who would raise Israel from the many deaths it had died, and bring about the Rule of God on earth. Their words of promise and hope are amongst the most memorable of Old Testament texts.

> Read Isaiah 9 : 1–7

> *The people who walked in darkness*
> *have seen a great light . . .*
> *A child is born to us!*
> *A son is given to us!*
> *And he will be our ruler.*
> *He will be called, 'Wonderful Counsellor',*
> *'Mighty God', 'Eternal Father',*
> *'Prince of Peace'.*
> *His royal power will continue to grow;*
> *his kingdom will always be at peace.*

> Read Isaiah 11 : 1–7

> *A new king will arise from among David's descendants . . .*
> *Wolves and sheep will live together in peace,*
> *and leopards will lie down with young goats.*
> *Calves and lion cubs will feed together,*
> *and little children will take care of them.*
> *Cows and bears will eat together,*
> *and their calves and cubs will lie down in peace.*

Words like these, full of hope and promise of peaceful deliverance from hostility, inspired Matthew. When he quotes from Jeremiah in the story of the massacre of the innocents (Matthew 2 : 18), he seems at first sight, to be making a deeply pessimistic comment. But if Matthew is referring his readers to the whole Jeremiah chapter, then he is pointing to one of the most hopeful chapters of the Old Testament. It is one in which Christians have most easily seen echoes of the New Testament.

> Read Jeremiah 31

Jeremiah, living over a hundred years after Isaiah, looked forward even more eagerly to a renewed Israel. The tears that Rachel shed at the Exile will stop. 'There is hope for your future.' (Jeremiah 31:17) There is to be a new covenant, not 'like the old covenant that I made with their ancestors when I took them by the hand and led them out of Egypt . . . The new covenant . . . will be this: I will put my law within them and write it on their hearts. I will be their God, and they will be my people.' (v.31–33)

Matthew and the early Christians saw all this fulfilled in Jesus. With his birth, another *exodus*, another *return from exile* was under way.

Questions and Things to Do

A   What do you know?

1   Which two Gospels have infancy stories?

2   On what day was Christmas originally celebrated?

3   In which town was Jesus born?

4   In which town did Jesus grow up?

5   Who was King of Judaea at the time of Jesus' birth?

6   What three gifts are the Magi said to have brought to the infant Jesus?

7   In chapters 1 and 2 dreams occur five times. When and to whom?

8   Name two prophets quoted by Matthew in the birth narrative.

9   Which Old Testament king was held in greatest regard by the Jews?

10   What is *midrash*?

B   What do you understand?

1   What does it mean to say that the birth stories in Matthew are theological rather than factual?

2   The five quotations in chapters 1 and 2 refer to five parts of the infancy drama. (a) Write out the quotations. (b) Describe the five parts of the infancy story to which they refer.

3   Why was the number fourteen significant to Matthew as he wrote his genealogy?

4   What has the Queen of Sheba to do with the story of the Magi?

5   Write a short essay on how Matthew used his infancy story to show Jesus to be a new David.

C   What do you think?

1   'Matthew may also intend his readers to dwell on the symbolic meaning of the gifts: gold has reference to royalty, frankincense to the prayer of adoration; myrrh to burial.' (Michael Fallon) Presume this was Matthew's intention and point out why *you* think these would be appropriate gifts for Jesus.

2   Outline two different interpretations of the 'virgin birth'. What does it mean to you? Give reasons for your view.

D   Things to do

1   Read the poem *Exceedingly Odd* (on the next page) and look up the Old Testament references.

2   Arrange a reading of T S Eliot's poem *The Journey of the Magi*, perhaps using background music. You might be able to do it at a school assembly at Christmastime.

3   Design your own Christmas card (according to Matthew).

4   Compose a ten-minute slide and music programme for the Christmas season. Try to use contemporary material.

Journey of the Magi

'A cold coming we had of it,
Just the worst time of the year
For a journey, and such a long journey:
The ways deep and the weather sharp,
The very dead of winter.
And the camels galled, sore-footed, refractory,
Lying down in the melting snow.
There were times we regretted
The summer palaces on slopes, the terraces,
And the silken girls bringing sherbet.
Then the camel men cursing and grumbling
And running away, and wanting their liquor and women,
And the night-fires going out, and the lack of shelters,
And the cities hostile and the towns unfriendly
And the villages dirty and charging high prices:
A hard time we had of it.
At the end we preferred to travel all night,
Sleeping in snatches,
With the voices singing in our ears, saying
That this was all folly.

Then at dawn we came down to a temperate valley,
Wet, below the snowline, smelling of vegetation,
With a running stream and a water-mill beating the darkness,
And three trees on the low sky,
And an old white horse galloped away in the meadow.
Then we came to a tavern with vine-leaves over the lintel,
Six hands at an open door dicing for pieces of silver,
And feet kicking the empty wine-skins.
But there was no information, so we continued
And arrived at evening, not a moment too soon
Finding the place; it was (you may say) satisfactory.

All this was a long time ago, I remember,
And I would do it again, but set down
This set down
This: were we led all that way for
Birth or Death? There was a Birth, certainly,
We had evidence and no doubt. I had seen birth and death,
But had thought they were different; this Birth was
Hard and bitter agony for us, like Death, our death.
We returned to our places, these Kingdoms,
But no longer at ease here, in the old dispensation,
With an alien people clutching their gods.
I should be glad of another death.'

T S Eliot
(Reprinted by permission of
Faber and Faber Ltd)

Exceedingly odd
are the means by which God
has provided our path to the heavenly shore.
Of the girls from whose line
the true light was to shine,
one was an adulteress, one was a whore.

There was Tamar who bore
—this we all must deplore—
a fine pair of twins to her father-in-law.
And Rahab the harlot;
her sins were as scarlet,
as red as the thread which she hung from her door.

But alone of her nation
she came to salvation,
and lived to be mother of Boaz of yore.
And he married Ruth,
a Gentile uncouth,
in a manner quite counter to biblical law.

And from her there did spring
blessed David the king,
who walked on his rooftop one evening, and saw
the wife of Uriah,
from whom he did sire
a baby that died—oh, and princes a score.

And a mother unmarried
it was too, who carried
God's Son, whom she laid in a cradle of straw,
that the upright might wait
at the heavenly gate,
while sinners and publicans go in before,
who have not earned their place,
but received it by grace,
and discovered a righteousness not of the Law.

Group of Ugandan teachers

TASK
Compose a Christmas carol

C3 Jesus, Son of God, Son of Man

Messenger from John

Father Gustavo Guttierez is Roman Catholic Professor of Theology in the Institute of Lima, Peru; he also looks after a slum parish in Lima. He recently addressed the Lambeth Conference (meeting of Anglican bishops) about the Church's option for the poor. He said: 'If we are not committed to the poor, we are in some way far from God. We must be committed to the poor not because the poor are good, but because God is good ... The beatitudes are not a revelation about the poor, but about God.' (Lambeth, 20th July 1988)

> *Read Matthew 11:1–6*

John the Baptist, now in prison, sends some disciples to ask Jesus if he is the expected Messiah. Maybe John was really expecting Jesus to be a preacher of fire, judgement, even retribution. For that was John's own style. Instead, John heard stories about Jesus' option for the poor.

Matthew's story is about Jesus, not about John (we don't hear what happens to him). Jesus says: 'Go back and tell John what you are hearing and seeing: the blind can see, the lame can walk ... and the Good News is preached to the poor.'

What did he mean by this answer?

> *Read Isaiah 35, especially verses 4–6*

The hope for the future expressed here is of another exodus through the desert towards Jerusalem. Everything would be transformed, the desert itself and the people.

The blind will be able to see

The blind will be able to see,
and the deaf will hear.
The lame will leap and dance,
and those who cannot speak will
shout for joy.   (v.5–6)

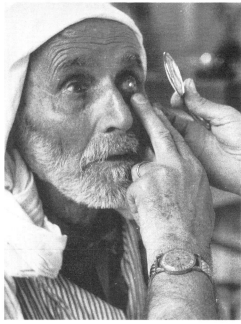

When Jesus gave his answer to John he was saying that these hopes were being realized. Matthew is quite clear about it. Jesus is the Messiah; he is taking people on the new exodus journey, towards the new Jerusalem. The miracles of Jesus were the signs that the transformation had begun, the Kingdom was at hand. Through his option for the poor Jesus was revealing God. Everything Jesus did was to reveal a God 'who is full of compassion and pity, ... who shows great love and faithfulness.' (Exodus 34:6)

Guttierez's message 'we must be committed to the poor ... because God is good' is very much at the heart of Matthew's Gospel. Jesus, as Matthew sees him, is the perfect expression that 'God is good'.

God's chosen servant

Anyone interested in classical music will be familiar with the story of the Passion in Handel's Messiah.

> *He was despised and rejected of men;*
> *a man of sorrows and acquainted with grief.*

The words of the aria are taken from the book of Isaiah.

Read Isaiah 53:1–12

Weighed down with suffering

They come at the end of a section of the book known as the Songs of the Suffering Servant. These are four poems about an ideal Israel, which has learnt through misunderstanding and suffering to become what God had always wanted it to be. It is an Israel which has outgrown early dreams of prosperity, and through suffering come to know an intimacy with God which only the poor and despised *can* appreciate. Such closeness to God is salvation. Priorities are right. The rejected and despised servant puts his trust in God. He is made the scapegoat and suffers *on behalf* of others. That is why

> *...he did not suffer in vain.*
> *My devoted servant, with whom I am pleased,*
> *will bear the punishment of many*
> *and for his sake I will forgive them.*   (v.11)

The poem has realized that a suffering Israel can be the salvation of others. This is a deep insight and forms the climax of a theme of suffering 'servants' in Old Testament literature—

Joseph, Moses, David, Jeremiah, and (at the time this poem was being written) the Exiles in Babylon.

It is hardly surprising that the early Christians saw the suffering and death of Jesus in the context of the Suffering Servant theme. Jesus was the ultimate fulfilment of this ideal Israel.

Matthew makes his *first* reference to this theme by quoting directly from the beginning of the first Suffering Servant poem, Isaiah 42:1–4.

Read Matthew 12:15–21

The chosen Servant is given his commission to establish justice on earth. He will do so in an unobtrusive way. His quiet 'option for the poor' will lead to suffering and eventually to his death.

Peter's declaration

Read Matthew 16:13–28

This scene is an important turning point in Matthew's Gospel. A disciple, Peter, speaks out and openly acknowledges Jesus as the Messiah—Christ. Matthew's train of thought is as follows:

1 *v.13–16* The long association of the disciples with Jesus has given them a deeper insight than other people share. Peter, spokesman for the rest, puts this insight into words.

2 *v.17–19* In response, Jesus commissions Peter to be the foundation stone of the community of believers.

3 *v.20* But this newly-discovered identity of Jesus is to remain a secret until its implications are unfolded.

4 *v.21* For the kind of Messiahship that Jesus claims involves suffering and death.

5 *v.22–23* Peter, human as he is, is horrified by the implications of such a Messiahship.

6 *v.24* To be a disciple of such a Messiah is equally horrifying—it also implies suffering, perhaps martyrdom.

Some details to notice:

1 *v.13–16* Matthew heightens the importance of Peter's statement by adding to Mark's declaration ('You are the Messiah') the further title 'the Son of the living God'. This is the way the post-resurrection community spoke of Jesus.

2 *v.17–19* These words to Peter are only recorded in Matthew. All the Gospels acknowledge the leading role of Peter. Matthew exphazises it. Here Peter is given authority to make pronouncements. Later (18:18) this authority is given to the whole Church. These two texts are the only ones in the Gospels to use the word 'church'.

3 *v.20* Commands to keep silent are much more frequent in Mark; Matthew retains only a few. (9:30, 12:16, 16:20 and 17:9.)

4 *v.21* Matthew's first specific prediction of Jesus' suffering and death. Presumably Jesus could foresee in general the outcome of his stand against the authorities. Presumably the evangelists developed less precise sayings of Jesus into clear predictions of death and resurrection.

5 *v.22–23* In v.18 Peter is a strong foundation rock. Here he is seen as a rock which blocks the path. His impulsive comment stands in the way of truth.

6 The section concludes with a reference to the Son of Man. Here the title means far more than in v.13, where it meant quite simply 'I, myself'. (See page 83.)

The Transfiguration

Read Matthew 17:1–13

Peter has proclaimed Jesus as Messiah. Jesus has replied that this will involve suffering. Naturally the disciples are bewildered. To help them understand, Peter, James and John are given a preview of the risen glory of Jesus. Matthew is preparing his readers for Jesus' death and for the connection between suffering and glory. 'Transfigure' means 'to change one's form'. The favoured disciples glimpsed Jesus in his resurrection state of glory.

Jesus and the three disciples go up a mountain where Jesus appears 'in light'. Elijah and Moses appear. Peter is so overcome that his comments are quite inappropriate. A cloud overshadows them and God's voice tells the disciples to listen to Jesus, his 'dear Son'.

The story is filled with Old Testament references. Matthew's first readers would easily be able to pick these up.

Details to notice

1   'Six days' may be a symbolic number. In the Sinai story, Moses spent six days in preparation before he was called to approach God in a Cloud. (Exodus 24:16)

2   Pilgrims celebrate this story on Mount Tabor in Galilee. Matthew was less interested in geography than in the significance of mountains. In the Old Testament, mountain tops were often the locations for supernatural revelations.

3   Moses and Elijah appear.

(a) *Moses*   Matthew sends his readers back to the occasion when Moses went up the mountain, wanting to see God's glory (Exodus 33:18). Moses was radiant after such close contact with God. Jesus too is transfigured by the glory of God. He is the new Moses.

(b) *Elijah* Matthew recalls that the prophet Elijah also wanted to
see the glory of God (1 Kings 19:8–13). He went to Mount Sinai,
where God revealed himself in a gentle whisper. Jesus is a new Elijah,
the prophet of God, the one promised. From now on everyone must
listen to him.

4   The glory-cloud reminds readers of the presence of God in the desert
(Exodus 13:21) and of the Baptism of Jesus (Matthew 3:17). The
rich symbolism of the scene is reinforced by the mention of tents.
Later Judaism saw the Feast of Tents (Tabernacles) as a reminder of
the lifestyle of the exodus people. Jesus leads the people of God in a
new exodus.

C4 The titles

Matthew uses a number of different titles for Jesus. He sees Jesus as:

1   Messiah (Hebrew) or Christ (Greek)

The word means 'anointed' or appointed by God for a special task. In this
sense, all the kings of Israel could be called messiahs. With the end of the
monarchy, the title began to be used for the future king who, it was
hoped, would restore Israel's former glory.
   'Simon Peter answered, "You are the Messiah."' (Matthew 16:16)

2   Son of David

Another title expressing the same hope.
   'Son of David! Take pity on us.' (Matthew 20:30)

3   Son of God

This title is also connected. The Israelite king was seen as God's 'Son' and
representative, enthroned at the right hand (south) of the Temple (see
Psalm 110:1). The title is, of course, capable of infinite expansion. Is
Jesus *a* son of God among others, or *the* unique Son of God?
   'He really was the Son of God!' (Matthew 27:54)

4   Son of Man

Another ambiguous title. At one extreme, it means no more that 'I
myself, a human being', and Matthew often uses it in this weak sense.
But at the other extreme, because of the use of this title by the book of
Daniel (7:13) and by later writers, 'Son of Man' came to mean a
heavenly person, hardly distinguishable from God himself, who would
descend to earth on a cloud to announce Kingdom Come. Did Jesus see
himself as fulfilling this exalted role?
   'The Son of Man is about to come in the glory of his Father with his
angels.' (Matthew 16:27)

5 Suffering Servant

The book of Isaiah describes, in four beautiful poems, the suffering entailed in being a faithful servant of God (see Isaiah 53 and page 80). The ideal Israel, the Old Testament says, will be vindicated by God and crowned with glory. Jesus, the New Testament says, fulfilled this role.

'Here is my servant, whom I have chosen.' (Matthew 12:18 = Isaiah 42:1)

6 Lord

The Greek 'kyrios' need mean no more than 'Mr' or 'Sir', and that is how it is still used in Greece today. But in the Greek Old Testament, '*The* Lord' was used to translate the name Yahweh, as the very title of God. The title was given to Jesus after the Resurrection, when it became a Christian profession of faith: 'Jesus is Lord.' Matthew easily gives Jesus this title before the Resurrection.

'Save me Lord!' he [Peter] cried.' (Matthew 14:30)

The titles Matthew gives to Jesus give us some idea of what the early Christians thought about him. They may therefore be taken as fair comment on the kind of person Jesus must have been. But they do not directly tell us how Jesus saw himself.

A What do you know?

1 Where was John the Baptist when he sent disciples to ask Jesus a question?

2 What was his question?

3 What was Jesus' answer?

4 Where in the Old Testament would you find the poems of the Suffering Servant?

5 Which disciple proclaimed: 'You are the Messiah, the Son of the Living God'?

6 Why did Jesus later say to this same disciple 'Get away from me Satan!'?

7 Which three disciples witnessed the Transfiguration?

8 Whom did the disciples see talking with Jesus on the mountain?

9 What is the Greek word for the Hebrew *Messiah*?

10 Give three titles used for Jesus.

B What do you understand?

1 Outline the theme of the Suffering Servant in the book of Isaiah. How is the theme applied to Jesus?

2 Why is the scene at Caesarea Philippi an important turning point in the Gospel?

3 Show how Matthew highlights the leading role given to Peter.

4 Outline the story of the Transfiguration. What do you understand the story to mean?

5 Why did Matthew use different titles to describe Jesus?

C What do you think?

The Lord says,
My servant will succeed in his task;
he will be highly honoured.
Many people were shocked when they saw him;
he was so disfigured that he hardly looked human.
But now many nations will marvel at him,
and kings will be speechless with amazement.
They will see and understand
something they have never known.

Isaiah 52:13–15

Read again Isaiah 53:1–12 and compare with Psalm 22.

1 'Many people turn to God in times of suffering.' Discuss.

2 Using *real* examples show how suffering can bring out the very best in people.

For Discussion

JESUS, HUMAN OR DIVINE?

When Kazantzakis' novel *The Last Temptation* (quoted on page 1) was made into a film by Scorsese it caused loud protest from Christians across the world. The author and film-producer were exploring the *humanity* of Jesus; to many it seemed to be at the expense of the *divinity*. Jesus, human or divine? human and divine? The question has perplexed, intrigued, and challenged people for nearly twenty centuries.

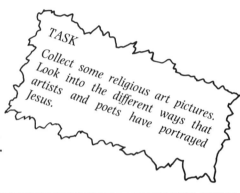

TASK

Collect some religious art pictures. Look into the different ways that artists and poets have portrayed Jesus.

If you are a son of man
You wonder where you're going,
And what will happen when you die,
There is no way of knowing.
They talk about a heaven
And they talk about a hell,
But whether they are right or not
No son of man can tell.

But if I were the son of God
And if they crucified me,
I'd think that I was luckier
Than those who hung beside me.
I'd know that I would rise again
And all things would be well.
But when you are a son of man
However can you tell?

If you are a son of man
Then you can be mistaken,
You hang upon the cross of doubt
You feel you are forsaken,
And whether you will rise again
Is more than you can tell.
And if you were the son of man
You've tasted this as well.

Sydney Carter
©*Stainer and Bell Ltd*

One of Sydney Carter's most famous songs, *Friday Morning*, discusses Jesus' divinity—'It's God they ought to crucify.' The song above discusses his humanity—'If you are a son of man.'
(Note that Carter uses the titles 'Son of God' and 'Son of Man' in the popular sense, not in the sense analyzed on page 83.)

C5 The passion and death of Jesus

Where is the cross?

I simply argue that the Cross be raised again at the centre of the market place as well as on the steeple of the church. I am recovering the claim that Jesus was not crucified in a cathedral between two candles, but on a cross between two thieves; on the town garbage heap; at a crossroad so cosmopolitan that they had to write his title in Hebrew and in Latin and in Greek (or shall we say in English, in Bantu and in Afrikaans?); at the kind of place where cynics talk smut, and thieves curse and soldiers gamble. Because that is where he died. And that is where churchmen should be and what churchmanship should be about.

George F Mcleod

Christians have always seen the cross as the clearest expression of what Christianity is about. Yet it confronts them with a problem. How could the man they recognize as the glorious Messiah have met such a shameful death—execution by crucifixion, alongside common criminals?

The first Christians tackled this problem head on. Their earliest writing about Jesus was probably an account of his Passion and death. Mark built his Gospel around it. Matthew used Mark's story and commented on it. The last section of his Gospel (chapters 26–28) begins and ends with words of Jesus. The drama that unfolds between is a stark account of the events. But it is dominated by two themes:

1   Jesus was throughout in complete control...he goes forward with clear knowledge of what is to come, and unswerving will to achieve it.

2   'These happenings were decreed by God from the beginning' (H Wansbrough). These two themes address the problem of the scandal of the cross. It is *above all* in Jesus' death, says Matthew, that the promise is fulfilled; Jesus is Messiah because of the cross.

Christians celebrate these last days of Jesus during 'Holy Week'—the week before Easter. How does Matthew tell the story?

The setting

Read Matthew 26:1–5

> In two days, as you know, it will be the Passover Festival and the Son of man will be handed over to be crucified.   (v.2)

Matthew sends his readers back to previous predictions of the Passion (16:21, 17:22, 20:18). Jesus' followers must not forget that he is the Son of Man—suffering yet finally victorious. He will die during the Passover season, when the Jews celebrate the deliverance of the nation from oppression. This is to be the new Passover.

The action starts straight away with the chief priests and elders plotting to put Jesus to death. Matthew places the conspiracy in Caiaphas' palace.

Jesus is anointed for burial

Read Matthew 26:6–13

For a Jew it was a terrible disgrace to be buried without being anointed. Jesus was spared this disgrace, because a woman (traditionally identified as Mary Magdalene) poured perfume over his head as he reclined at Simon's table. The disciples (John's Gospel makes Judas their spokesman) complain about the waste.

Here is how Sydney Carter retells the story.

Said Judas to Mary, 'Now what will you do
With your ointment so rich and so rare?'
'I'll pour it all over the feet of my Lord,
And I'll wipe it away with my hair,' she said,
'I'll wipe it away with my hair.'

'O Mary, O Mary, O think of the poor —
This ointment, it could have been sold!
And think of the blankets and think of the bread
You could buy with the silver and gold,' he said,
'You could buy with the silver and gold.'

'Tomorrow, tomorrow, I'll think of the poor,
Tomorrow,' she said, 'not today.
For dearer than all of the poor in the world,
Is my love who is going away,' she said,
'Is my love who is going away.'

Said Jesus to Mary: 'Your love is so deep,
Today you may do as you will.
Tomorrow, you say, I am going away,
But my body I leave with you still,' he said,
'My body I leave with you still.'

'The poor of the world are my body,' he said,
'To the end of the world they shall be;
And the bread and the blankets you give to the poor
You'll find you have given to me,' he said,
'You'll find you have given to me.'

'The poor of the world are my body'

Jesus praises the woman because 'What she did was . . . to get me ready for burial.' (Matthew 26:12) In Luke's and John's account the oil is poured on his feet. Matthew follows Mark, and tells of the oil being poured over Jesus' head, as over a king. For Matthew, Jesus is *The Anointed One* (Christ). He is saying that Jesus became the Christ in his death.

Judas agrees to betray Jesus

> *Read Matthew 26:14–16*

In sharp contrast to the woman's generosity Matthew now tells of Judas' greed. Far from spending himself on Jesus, he hopes to profit from Jesus' death. Mark had mentioned money—Matthew puts a price on it: 'thirty silver coins.'' Matthew has in mind a text in the book of Zechariah. God's plan is carried out even in Judas' treachery. (See Zechariah 11:12.)

Jesus and the authorities are now set on a collision course. The sequence of events that follows is very familiar to Christians who follow the Holy Week/Easter liturgy (worship).

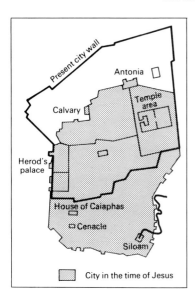

City in the time of Jesus

Sequence of Events

1 Passover meal
2 Jesus predicts Peter's denial
3 Jesus prays in Gethsemane and is arrested
4 Jesus before the Council
5 Peter denies Jesus
6 Judas commits suicide
7 Jesus is taken to Pilate and questioned
8 Jesus is sentenced to death and mocked by soldiers
9 Jesus is crucified and dies
10 Jesus is buried

Jerusalem today

1 Passover meal

Read Matthew 26:17–30

The Passover was (and remains today) the 'birthday-feast' of the Jewish nation. Celebrated at full moon in the month of Nisan (March–April), it is a festival of freedom, and commemorates God's liberation of Israel from Egyptian slavery. The feast is celebrated for a whole week and is also known as the Festival of Unleavened Bread.

In Jesus time, as today, many Jews travelled to Jerusalem to celebrate the feast. Under Roman occupation, mob violence was not unusual. This is the scene that forms the background to the last week of Jesus' life. Nervous of political riots, the authorities gratefully accept Judas' help.

Mark had told the story of the preparation of the Passover meal with lively detail. Matthew trims it down to give only the outline. Even his description of the meal itself is condensed, and shows no interest in the details of the Passover celebrations. He assumes his readers can fill them in. His only interest is in the fact that Jesus chose the Passover setting for his last meal with his friends.

When people die, their families often look back with particular emotion to the last occasion when they had a meal together. The early church so treasured the last meal Jesus ate with his disciples that it became the focal point of their worship. They re-enacted the Passover meal in a stylized way. This has become the central worship of the Christian church. It is known as the Mass, the Communion Service or the Eucharist (thanksgiving).

Newly ordained ministers of the Church of Ireland. Ministers in the churches are appointed on behalf of the community to lead the Communion Service or Eucharist.

Bread of life

Points to Notice about the Meal

1   Read Exodus 12:21–28 for the Passover background. Notice the
    shedding of blood as a sign of the Covenant between God and his
    people.
2   Matthew (following Mark) sees the meal as a sacred ritual. Jesus'
    words are reduced to the ritual formula already adopted in church
    worship. (See 1 Corinthians 11:24–25, written twenty years earlier.)
3   Nonetheless, the words follow the pattern of the Jewish Passover.
    Just as the Jewish head of the family said, 'This unleavened bread *is*
    (and brings into the present) our Egyptian slavery,' so Jesus says,
    'This broken bread *is* my broken body; this poured wine *is* (and
    brings into the present) my bloodshed.'
4   Those who eat the Passover meal share in its meaning. Those who
    eat Jesus' last supper volunteer to share Jesus' self-sacrifice.
5   Matthew adds the explanation that Jesus' 'blood is poured out for the
    forgiveness of sins'.

2   Jesus predicts Peter's Denial

Read Matthew 26:31–35

After the supper Jesus and the disciples go out towards the Mount of
Olives. Jesus tells them that the text of Zechariah: 'God will kill the
shepherd, and the sheep of the flock will be scattered' will again be
fulfilled that night—for he will be arrested whilst they run away. Peter
objects, but Jesus predicts that he will deny him three times before cock-
crow. Peter and the disciples continue to protest their loyalty.

3   Jesus prays in Gethsemane and is arrested

Read Matthew 26 : 36–56

Matthew here follows Mark very closely. Jesus goes to pray at a place on the Mount of Olives called Gethsemane, which means 'the oil-press'. His anguish and distress contrast starkly with the unsuspecting and un-caring sleep of the three disciples, Peter, James and John, who don't come out of the story very well. Perhaps Peter told the story against himself. On the other hand the historical accuracy of the story is doubtful. Many commentators point out that *sleeping* disciples could not witness Jesus' actual prayer.

The triple prayer is a recognizable literary device to stress per-severance. The words are in the spirit of the Psalms. Matthew adds the words 'your will be done' (v.42), a phrase from the 'Lord's Prayer' (see Matthew 6:10 and page 19). Jesus is portrayed as showing by example how Christians in similar distress should pray.

Jesus prays three times. The disciples sleep three times. Jesus has predicted that Peter will deny him three times.

Whilst Jesus is speaking to his bewildered disciples a crowd arrives led by Judas Iscariot. He greets Jesus with the kiss with which a disciple would greet his rabbi. This was the agreed signal for the soldiers to make their arrest.

The betrayal of Jesus by an apostle, the clumsy action of a disciple to defend Jesus, the fact that the disciples finally run away scared—all this throws into sharp relief the loneliness of Jesus. Yet he remains in total control of events.

Matthew adds the proverbial saying 'All who take the sword will die by the sword' (v.52), a quotation from God's covenant with Noah. (Genesis 9:6)

4   Jesus before the Council

Read Matthew 26 : 57–68

According to Matthew, there is no formal trial of Jesus by the Jews, only an interrogation during the night at the house of Caiaphas. The chief priests, elders and teachers who make up the Council (Sanhedrin), meet in order to find a cause to send Jesus to Pilate. They can't find any obvious offence to charge him with. Jesus maintains a dignified silence. Matthew still has the Suffering Servant in mind: 'He was treated harshly, but endured it humbly; he never said a word.' (Isaiah 53:7)

The High Priest finally challenges Jesus to admit to being the Messiah. But he refuses to accept the title in the sense suggested. He claims to be something far greater—the Son of Man, the glorious figure of Daniel's vision. (See Daniel 7:13 and page 83.) His listeners regard this as blasphemy. Now they have a charge to make against him. The Councillors mock and abuse Jesus.

5   Peter denies Jesus

Read Matthew 26:69–75

Matthew now returns to Peter, still outside in the courtyard. Two servant girls and a bystander recognize him as a companion of Jesus. Frightened by the turn of events he denies all knowledge of Jesus. On the third denial he remembers what Jesus had predicted, and bursts into tears.

6   Judas commits suicide

Read Matthew 27:3–10

The interval between the Council's decision and the trial before Pilate allows Matthew to tell us about Judas' death (Luke alone has a parallel story in Acts). Matthew, as ever, only tells the story to show how it fitted certain Old Testament texts. Judas repents of his treachery and returns the money. The Council are unsympathetic; Judas throws the coins in the Temple and hangs himself. The priests can't use such tainted money for the Temple, so they buy land for a cemetery. This, says Matthew, fulfils a text of Jeremiah. But the text he quotes is actually from the book of Zechariah, to which Matthew seems to be partial. (Zechariah 11:12–13)

7 Jesus is taken to Pilate and questioned

Read Matthew 26 : 1–2 and 27 : 11–14

Early in the morning the priests and elders make their plans. They are determined to do away with Jesus, but have not got the authority to impose the death penalty. So he must be taken to the Roman Governor Pilate, with a newly fabricated political charge that Rome will take seriously. Pilate asks him 'Are you the King of the Jews?' Presumably this is now the accusation. A claim of kingship would be an act of treason. Jesus avoids a direct answer and resumes his silence.

8 Jesus is sentenced to death and is mocked by soldiers

Read Matthew 27 : 15–31

Although Jesus was executed by the Romans, Matthew puts the blame squarely on the Jewish leaders. He even represents the Roman Governor three times attempting to release Jesus. But Pilate is no match for the priests and elders, and finally gives in to their demands for the death sentence.

So Jesus is flogged (the usual preliminary of crucifixion), and handed over to the Roman soldiers. They find the accusation of 'kingship' hilarious and dress Jesus as a mock king, with a soldier's scarlet cloak to represent the kingly robe, a crown of thorn twigs, and a reed for a sceptre. In the excavations of the Antonia fortress, in Jerusalem, a courtyard pavement reveals a soldiers' game scratched on the stone. The letters and figures form a kind of snakes and ladders game to make fun of a mock king. Perhaps they played this game on Jesus.

A soldiers' game scratched on the pavement

Matthew adds two incidents to the account he has borrowed from Mark.

1 Pilate's wife warns her husband of Jesus' innocence because of a dream. Matthew often uses dreams as a sign of the mysterious presence of God.
2 Pilate disclaims responsibility with the symbolic action of washing his hands. The responsibility lies on the Jews and their descendants. Matthew has seen the destruction of Jerusalem 40 years later, and interpreted it as God's punishment for Jewish guilt. Tragically, Matthew's interpretation sowed the seeds for future centuries of anti-Semitism.

9   Jesus is crucified and dies

Read Matthew 27 : 32–56

The crucifixion   Matthew, like Mark, is very brief in his description of Jesus' last hours. The entire account of Jesus' death is almost impersonal in its dignified restraint.

Simon, a North African, is forced to help Jesus carry his cross. The soldiers offer Jesus a drug to alleviate the pain, but he refuses it. Jesus is crucified, and the soldiers gamble for his clothes. The accusation 'The King of the Jews' is posted up for everyone to see. Two terrorists are crucified beside him. They insult and taunt Jesus, as do the Jewish bystanders.

Matthew only makes small changes to Mark's text; he does so to emphasize two themes:
1   Everything is to fulfil the Old Testament—the wine mixed with gall, the gambling for clothes, sharing the fate of criminals, the mockery of the bystanders.
    Read again Psalms 22 and 69 to see the texts Matthew has in mind.
2   The greatest hostility is shown by the Jewish authorities and by- standers. Matthew places the blame on them.

The death of Jesus   Matthew follows Mark in describing Jesus' death in terms of cosmic disturbances, to mark the beginning of a new age. Darkness from noon till 3 pm may recall one of the plagues before the exodus. Jesus cries out 'My God, my God, why did you abandon me?', the shattering opening words of Psalm 22, but the rest of the Psalm is full of hope and trust in God. Jesus dies. The Temple curtain is torn in two—the barrier between God and the world is broken down. Matthew adds even more symbolic signs: an earthquake and the dead rising from their graves. Matthew underlines his belief that here God has intervened to inaugurate a new creation.

The centurion and his soldiers are terrified by the earthquake. The centurion unwittingly proclaims the truth for Matthew: 'He really was the Son of God.'

Matthew concludes the scene by mentioning the women who watched from a distance. They fulfil another Old Testament text, Psalm 38; and they provide a link with the story of the resurrection which follows.

10   Jesus is buried

Read Matthew 27 : 57–66

According to Jewish Law (Deuteronomy 21:22) a body could not be left hanging overnight after execution. Joseph of Arimathea, a disciple (Mark says he was an official), bravely volunteers to bury Jesus. He prepares the body for burial in a clean shroud, and places it in his own unused tomb. He rolls a stone across the doorway. Mary Magdalene and another Mary witness the burial.

Only Matthew tells the story of guards at the tomb (he returns to them later, see 28:4, 11–15).

C6   The meaning of Jesus' death

It seems a paradox that Christians call the day of Jesus' death, *Good Friday*. How can a death be good news? Over the centuries, Christian thinkers have tried to explain the significance of the Cross. They have tried to turn to metaphors to explore their insights, and have spoken of

> God as a judge in a lawcourt needing to deal out his justice, or
> of a legal contract needing to be kept, or
> of slaves needing to be brought out of slavery, or
> of an angry master needing to be calmed, or
> of God's rights needing to be recognized by the slaughter of lambs.

These metaphors were used, especially in the Middle Ages, to help people make sense of Jesus' death. They linger on in some of the old hymns. One hymn speaks of

That spotless lamb, *who more than due,*
paid *for his sheep, and that sheep you, Alleluia.*
That guiltless Son, who bought *your peace,*
And made his Father's anger *cease, Alleluia.*
                              Wipo (11th century) tr. Walter Kirkham Blount

Few of these metaphors speak clearly to people in the 20th century. Today's Christians have been guided by recent theologians back to the Evangelists. How did *they* see the death of Jesus?

For Mark, Jesus death is simply the inevitable fate of a spokesman for God. All Christians are called to similar martyrdom. After all, Mark was writing during the Roman persecutions.

Matthew wrote at a later time when Christians were tolerated. He inevitably reinterpreted the meaning of the Cross. For him it is the necessary agony before the birth of a new age. The Suffering Servant must die, as the Old Testament had predicted. But with earth-shattering signs, a new world is born. A new Israel emerges out of the old, led by a new Moses. The resurrection stories will confirm this.

A   What do you know?

1   In what way was Jesus anointed for his burial?

2   For what price did Judas agree to betray Jesus?

3   When is the Passover celebrated?

4   What does the Passover commemorate?

5   Where was Jesus arrested?

6   Who were the Council (Sanhedrin)?

7   What did the priests do with the money Judas returned?

8   Who was the Roman Governor?

9   According to Matthew, what were Jesus' last words?

10   According to Matthew, what signs accompanied Jesus' death?

B   What do you understand?

1   Outline the story of the woman anointing Jesus with perfume. Why did Matthew place the story at this part of the Gospel?

2   In what way did Matthew see the Last Supper of Jesus as a new Passover?

3   Describe the part Judas Iscariot played in the drama.

4   In what aspects of the passion story does Matthew see Jesus as the Suffering Servant of Isaiah?

5   Show some of the ways in which Matthew puts the blame for Jesus' death on to the Jewish authorities.

C   What do you think?

1   Describe the scene in the garden of Gethsemane before the arrest. Do you think it can be historically accurate? What do you think happened there?

2   Imagine you are Pilate and retell the trial scene from his point of view. Explain the reasons for 'your' decision to have Jesus crucified.

3   'We are not carrying the cross when we are poor or sick—these are all parts of life. The cross comes when we try to change things. That is how it came for Jesus'.' Fr Miguel D'Escoto, Nicaraguan Foreign Minister. Write an essay to open out this reflection.

D   Things to do

1   Collect different pictures of Christ on the cross and display them.

2   Write out Psalm 22 and Isaiah 53. Illustrate them both with contemporary photos/newspaper cuttings.

3   Prepare a public reading of Matthew's passion, using music and slides.

4   Design a cross which symbolizes contemporary suffering.

5   Write your own psalm to express anguish or sorrow.

You passed a resolution on the morning that I died;
You established a committee on the day my mother cried;
You deplored how the hungry of the world must waste away,
How the refugee is homeless at the ending of the day.
Your voting was unanimous, you all gave your assent
To investigate my hunger on the day my hunger went.
My hunger went on the day that I died
And in my death your Lord was crucified.

You preached a brilliant sermon on the day I passed away,
As my soul went home to Glory I could clearly hear you say
How in Matthew chapter twenty-five it says to love the poor;
Your three main points were all designed to make the
conscience soar.
Your dictation it was faultless as you said just what you
meant;
But you preached about my hunger on the day my hunger went.
My hunger went on the day that I died
And in my death your Lord was crucified.

But there are many like me who have yet a while to live
And you are not alone in having so much you can give,
Your sermons and committees will not take my pain away—
You'll need a better tale than that to tell on Judgment Day.
God lent you wealth to share with me, while to your Government
He gave the power to save my life—the day my hunger went.
My hunger went on the day that I died
And in my death your Lord was crucified.
David Goodbourn

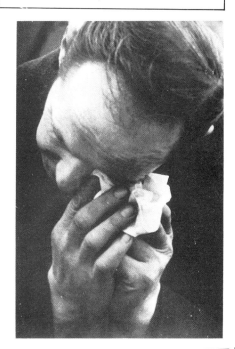

DEATH

There are many reasons behind famine in Africa. There's intense poverty, which means people can't adopt the necessary measures to fight drought. There's internal struggles and conflicts. There's a lack of consistent co-ordinated external aid. And in the case of Angola and Mozambique there's the effects of South Africa's policies of sabotage and de-stabilisation. In each area the causes vary.

The result is always the same: death. The death of thousands upon thousands of innocent victims.

But Trócaire is helping the people of Africa. Tackling the causes of hunger. Implementing long-term development programmes. And above all, working towards justice for all. Trócaire needs your support.

STREETWISE IN BRAZIL

Children sleeping rough in the streets of Rio

GO TO PRACA DEODORO, the main square of Maceio in Brazil's north-east, any evening and you'll find hundreds of 'street kids'. Some have been sent there by their families, many are completely homeless. They all take any opportunity they can to get something for themselves and their families' daily bread — carrying and loading, scavenging, hawking, washing cars, stealing.

. . . there are estimated to be more than 50 million 'street children' in Latin America today.

Oxfam has just approved a new grant for work with street children in Brazil. A church based group of teachers and street workers makes regular contact with children. They aim to channel their energies into learning skills which will give them a more stable income. And to build their confidence and self-respect. Many are also being shown a way back into the state school system.

Most important, they help provide what the children themselves say they want — food, learning, care and affection.

A tall order for those who do care — there are estimated to be more than 50 million street children in Latin America today.

See over for news from Kampuchea · Namibia · Zaire ▶

C7 The resurrection

> **Resurrection**
> It was night in the basement
> Of a shuttered building
>
> Those wounded by the atomic bomb
> Filled up the dark basement
> Without light of a single candle
> Amid the smell of blood
> The stench of dead bodies
> A sweaty stuffiness—and a sound of moaning
> Out of them, a strange voice was heard:
>
> 'A baby is being born.'
>
> In the hell of the basement like this
> A young woman is in labour at this moment
> What should the people do
> In this darkness, without a match?
> The people huddled there
> Were anxious about her
> Forgetting their own pain
> Then—
> A voice sounded, 'I am a midwife!
> I will assist at the birth!'
> It was a severely wounded person
> Who spoke, one who had been moaning
> A moment ago. Thus in the dark
> In the bottom of the hell, a new life
> Came into the world. The midwife
> Died before dawn, covered with blood
> Let it be born! Let it be born!
> Even if one must pay with one's own life.
>
> Sadako Kurihara

Out of the suffering and death—a new life. This is *resurrection*.

Resurrection means life triumphing over death. There is a resurrection whenever goodness and love triumph over evil and hatred. Is the story of Jesus' resurrection any different from this? Jesus died as a criminal, shattering the hearts and hopes of his disciples. They knew despair. Then something happened to dispel their darkness. This is how Matthew describes it.

> After the Sabbath, as Sunday morning was dawning, Mary Magdalene and the other Mary went to look at the tomb. Suddenly there was a violent earthquake; an angel of the Lord came down from heaven, rolled the stone away, and sat on it. His appearance was like lightning, and his clothes were as snow. The guards were so afraid that they trembled and became like dead men.
> The angel spoke to the women. 'You must not be afraid,' he said. 'I know you are looking for Jesus, who was crucified. He is not here; he has been raised, just as he said. Come here and see the place where he was lying. Go quickly now, and tell his disciples, "He has been raised from death, and now he is going to Galilee ahead of you; there you will see him!" Remember what I have told you.'
> Matthew 28:1–7

Something extraordinary took place at the weekend following Jesus'
death. It changed the whole course of events; it transformed the disciples. This does not mean that the events themselves were of the kind
that could have been filmed. Perhaps we will never know exactly what
happened. Read Matthew's presentation of the resurrection stories. His
account is in three parts:

1   The two women at the tomb. (28:1–10)
2   The report of the guard. (28:11–15)
3   Jesus appears to the disciples. (28:16–20)

1   The two women at the tomb

Compare Matthew's story with the accounts in the other Gospels:
Mark 16:1–8, Luke 24:1–12, John 20:1–10. Notice the details on
which the accounts differ. To get a single coherent account, the texts
would need to be twisted about, and awkward details left out. This will
become even more obvious to anyone who tries to make a single account
of the appearance stories that follow.

*'Mary Magdalene and the
other Mary went to look at
the tomb'* Matthew 28:1

   In the past people simply tried to string all these stories together in
sequence, presuming they were straightforward reports of what happened.
Today commentators presume that they were never meant as factual
descriptions of observable events, but simply stories in which people
expressed what resurrection meant to them.
   Matthew's story doesn't centre on the empty tomb—his women don't
accept the invitation to inspect it. The emphasis is on the angel's
message pointing to Galilee. It prepares the reader for the climax of the
Gospel—the last scene in Galilee where Jesus will give his commission to
the eleven. The angel and the earthquake are both used by Matthew (as
elsewhere in Scripture) to say in picture language, 'God was in this
event.'

2   The report of the guard

Matthew is alone in mentioning guards at the tomb. This is odd. There is no trace of them in Matthew's source (Mark), nor in the Gospels that were written later by Luke and John. Did Matthew invent this detail in order to refute contemporary Jewish slanders that the resurrection stories were based on a body stolen from the tomb? If so, it would be a good example of the freedom with which the Evangelists used stories to emphasize that, for them, the resurrection was neither fraud nor fantasy, but something real.

Scripture scholars today suggest that the *empty tomb* may be part of the same free use of story. All four Gospels speak of a tomb miraculously emptied, so presumably the story is based on very early tradition. Yet strangely, the earliest New Testament reference to the resurrection makes no mention of it, only of the appearance of Jesus to his friends. Paul, writing to Christians in Corinth in AD56 (ten years before Mark wrote, twenty years before Matthew), says:

> *I passed on to you what I received, which is of the greatest importance: that Christ died for our sins, as written in the Scriptures; that he was buried and that he was raised to life three days later, as written in the Scriptures; that he appeared to Peter, and then to all twelve apostles. Then he appeared to more than five hundred of his followers at once, most of whom are still alive, although some have died. Then he appeared to James, and afterwards to all the apostles. Last of all he appeared also to me...*   1 Corinthians 15:3–8

Did Paul simply assume that Jesus' tomb must have been empty, and that this was not worth mentioning? Or did he regard the image of an empty tomb as a highly *dramatic* way of saying that, after Easter day, it was no good looking for Jesus in a Jerusalem cemetery? He is now to be found only in the midst of his friends. This is a reality that cannot be photographed.

Paul never knew Jesus while he was alive. He only 'met' him when he was converted to Christianity on the Damascus road, in the midst of a journey that was meant to put an end to Christianity. He describes this experience as 'seeing Jesus' (1 Corinthians 9:1), and 'hearing' Jesus say, 'Why do you persecute me?' (Acts 9:5). Clearly, such a Jesus is now to be found only in the Christian community.

3   Jesus appears to the Disciples

Paul's claim, that he had 'seen' the risen Jesus just as really as the first disciples did, should make us cautious about making black and white judgements on Jesus' resurrection appearances. All the Gospels make the strongest possible claims that his friends 'saw' him alive in their midst after death. But was this a physical sighting that could have been videoed, or an *insight* into the fact that his death was not the end of him? The second kind of 'sight' is no less real than the first.

Matthew makes much of Jesus' final appearance to his disciples. He describes it, as he has described all that Jesus did, in terms of Old Testament texts.

1   Jesus appears on a mountain, as God did to Moses (Exodus 3:6–12). He is received with the same sense of awe and hesitation. But he also gives the same assurance, 'I will be with you.'

2   Jesus is at the same time the new Moses, close to God, teaching the new Israel to obey everything 'he has commanded' them (Deuteronomy 5:31–33).

3   Jesus is the supreme Prophet, given 'authority over nations and kingdoms' as Jeremiah was (Jeremiah 1:8–10). This text also uses the words, 'I will be with you.'

4   Jesus is the Son of Man ('a human being' according to the Good News Bible) who is given 'authority, honour and royal power, so that the people of all nations . . . would serve him' (Daniel 7:14).

By weaving these texts together, Matthew evokes a strong sense of fulfilment. For him, Jesus' death and resurrection form the climax of God's plans.

The scene is Matthew's construction. This is made very clear by the baptism-formula of v.19. This formula was unlikely to have been taught by Jesus. The earliest baptisms we read of were done simply 'in the name of Jesus Christ'. (Acts 2:38) Baptism 'in the name of the Father, Son and Holy Spirit' was the liturgical practice of Matthew's own time.

Matthew is alone in placing this scene on a mountain in Galilee, which is where he had placed Jesus' earthly teaching. But what had been spoken there only to Jews is now broadcast to the whole Gentile world. With this sense of completion Matthew is able to end the Gospel where he began it. On his first page (1:23) he had called Jesus Immanuel—'God is with us.' On this last page Jesus promises 'I will be with you.' His readers are assured that, in the risen Jesus, God is with them for all time.

Questions and Things to Do

A What do you know?

1 According to Matthew, who visited the tomb on Sunday morning?

2 In the angel's message, what were the disciples told to do?

3 What was the reaction of the women?

4 What was the message of Jesus to the women?

5 According to Matthew, who reported the resurrection to the chief priests?

6 What report was 'spread round by the Jews to this very day'?

7 Who was converted to Christianity on the Damascus Road?

8 According to Matthew where did Jesus appear to his disciples?

9 What was the reaction of the disciples to this resurrection appearance?

10 In the final instruction to the disciples, Jesus uses words from the liturgy of Matthew's day. What are they?

B What do you understand?

1 Describe the visit of the women to the tomb as Matthew records it.

2 Point out some of the differences in the way Mark and Matthew write of the resurrection.

3 What is the significance of earthquakes for Matthew?

4 What did Paul say about the resurrection which suggests that 'resurrection' is about *insight* rather than about *sightings*?

C What do you think?

1 Describe Matthew's account of the appearance of Jesus to the disciples. In what way is it a fitting summary of his Gospel?

2 Describe three occasions where mountains feature in Matthew's narrative. Can you account for his interest in mountains?

3 Do Christians have to take the resurrection stories as literal descriptions of historical fact? What do you think really happened?

4 'A Christian is one who believes that Jesus lives on in the community. His death was not the end of the story, but the beginning of it.' What do you think this means?

D Things to do

1 Collect stories from magazines, newspapers, or from your own experience, which illustrate love triumphing over death, hatred or fear.

2 Make a collage (using any medium) to illustrate resurrection.

3 Can you find stories which have a resurrection theme: (a) in other world religions (b) in children's literature (c) in folklore?

> The resurrection did not result in a committee with a chairman, but in a fellowship with an experience.

New life in unexpected places

Christ in Szezed

Christ in the World suddenly took on a new meaning this month. I have returned this week from an international workshop on inter-cultural communication at Szezed in Hungary. Religion was not mentioned – nor God – but Christ was there in a world of contradictions and struggle and pain and love as 250 people from almost all the countries of Eastern and Western Europe and also Israel and the U.S.A. met for a week in an unstructured community – striving to meet and communicate person to person.

The workshop was the dream of an American therapist called Carl Rogers (who is now 82) to whom both adult education and counselling and group work owe great debts.

Carl Rogers's work has a lot to teach some communities in the Church. People can work in new and creative ways. Two hundred and fifty people can be trusted and facilitated to work with no agenda, no speakers, no structure for three hours each day for a week and the learning can be enormous because it comes out of the experience itself and for me it puts me in touch with the deepest part of myself. I know I have come back changed. I know Christ is in the world in unexpected contexts. I know that the Christ in me has been in touch with the pain and the joy of the world. And we never mentioned God.

RESURRECTION

There is a story told of an assistant of the great scientist, Faraday. One day he knocked a little silver cup into a jar of acid. Almost immediately, it disappeared, eaten by the acid. When Faraday came in, he added some chemicals to the acid and instantly, the silver particles sank to the bottom of the jar. He then sifted them out and sent the mass of silver particles to a friend who was a silversmith. Soon the cup was restored again, shining and brighter than ever.

If Faraday the scientist and a silversmith could do that, then I have no difficulty believing that God can gather together the scattered dust of His people and resurrect them in power and glory to shine with the image of His own Dear Son.

"Behold I show you a mystery; we shall not all sleep, but we shall all be changed. In a moment, in the twinkling of an eye, at the last trump: for the trumpet shall sound, and the dead shall be raised incorruptible, and we shall be changed." 1 Cor 15:51-52.

One day, when my sufferings were at their worst, I was listening to the Seventh Symphony (Beethoven), and suddenly, as the woodwind announced the lovely, tranquil theme of the Trio to the Scherzo, I felt the load drop from me, as did Bunyan's Pilgrim before the Cross. 'Fear no more,' said the Trio; 'fear no more! Underneath are the everlasting arms.' The relief and reassurance were deep and sweet; and, although the cure had only begun, its power increased steadily. From that moment I could always recapture the renovating virtue by thinking of that Trio.

Basil Willey

Voice of the voiceless

In the story of Salvador you must always speak of Archbishop Romero. Chosen as archbishop because he was considered a safe bet, a man who'd never rock the boat, he became a changed man when one of his priests was murdered. It was like a sudden conversion. From that moment, Romero became the voice of the voiceless. Nothing stopped him from speaking out. In 1980 he appealed to the Salvadorean soldiers 'I beg you to obey your consciences, not your commanding officers. I implore you to stop the repression.' Next day he was shot dead in his cathedral. That voice could no longer be allowed to speak in Salvador because he was speaking the truth. Romero knew the danger he was in. He said, 'If they kill me, I will rise again in the people of Salvador'. And that is what is happening now.

Extended Question

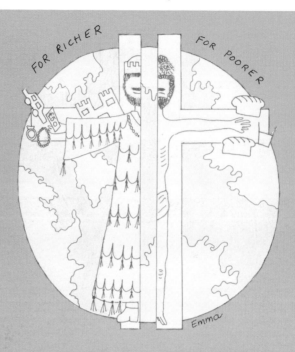

I am so glad to be a Christian and that the God whom we worship is one who cares that people are hungry, that they are discriminated against, that, in South Africa they are uprooted and dumped in forlorn, poverty-stricken places as if they were rubbish. God cares; if he did not, I for one would not worship him. God is the hope of the downtrodden, of the exploited, of the powerless—because he is always biased in their favour...Praise be to him forever and ever.

Archbishop Desmond Tutu

1   Why is Archbishop Tutu glad to be a Christian? (1)

2   What would cause the Archbishop to stop worshipping God? (1)

3   What is Emma 'saying' in her picture of the cross? (4)

4   Describe (a) the situation of one group of people (anywhere in the world) who are innocent victims of suffering; (b) the help offered to them. (6)

5   Do you think a Christian should become involved in political struggle to overcome injustice? (4)

6   Resurrection is 'Life out of Death'. Choose a healing miracle from the Gospel and show how it is really a resurrection story. (4)

Useful Addresses

Cross Group 6A Cumberland Park, Dundonald, Belfast BT16 0AY (Support group for bereaved in N Ireland)

174 Trust 174 Antrim Road, Belfast BT15 2AJ (service to inner city)

Protestant & Catholic Encounter 103 University Street, Belfast BT7 1HP

Justice and Peace Commission (RC) 28 Rose Street, Glasgow G3 6RE

The Leonard Cheshire Foundation 26–29 Maunsel Street, London SW1P 2QN

Concern 1 Upper Camden Street, Dublin 2

Useful Reading

Sheila Cassidy *Audacity to Believe* Fount 1978

Shirley du Boulay *Cicely Saunders: The Founder of the Modern Hospice Movement* Hodder & Stoughton 1984

The Community

D1   Matthew and his community

We've now seen the life and death of Jesus through Matthew's eyes. The way he has told the story gives us some clues about who Matthew was—a Jewish scribe, devoted to his Bible, who had become a thoughtful Christian. There may even be an autobiographical note in Matthew 13:52: 'Every teacher of the Law (scribe) who becomes a disciple in the Kingdom of heaven is like the owner of a house who takes new and old things out of his storeroom.'

This is exactly what Matthew does.

1   He takes *old* texts and ideas from the Scriptures and interweaves them into his story of Jesus.
2   He tells the story of Jesus in the light of his *new* post-resurrection experience of Christian community life.

Jesus is the centre of Matthew's world; the fulfilment of the past, the meaning of the present, the hope of the future.

D2 Jesus and the Old Testament people of God

Matthew was a Jew by birth. His whole understanding of God was rooted in his Jewish history. For him, Jesus was the climax of that history, and its best interpreter. The story of the Old Testament People of God could be understood in terms of:

The Law   (Part 1 of this book, pages 5 to 34)

Under the leadership of Moses a ragged group of nomads became a *people*. He convinced them that they were chosen and special. At Mount Sinai they entered into a covenant with God, agreeing to live by his laws.

> Read Exodus 19:1–8

> *Now, if you will obey me and keep my covenant, you will be my own people. The whole earth is mine, but you will be my chosen people, a people dedicated to me alone, and you will serve me as priests . . . All the people answered together, 'We will do everything that the Lord has said.'* (v.5, 8)

The Prophets   (Part 2 of this book, pages 35 to 68)

All the Old Testament prophets saw themselves as stand-ins for Moses. They were Israel's conscience, reminding people of their failure to live up to the promise made at Mt Sinai. Their disastrous history showed how often they had failed. But things could be different, because God's love was stronger than their weakness. The Prophet Jeremiah puts this in memorable words:

> Read Jeremiah 31:31–34

> *The new covenant that I will make with the people of Israel will be this: I will put my law within them and write it on their hearts. I will be their God, and they will be my people.* (v.33)

The Promised Liberator   (Part 3 of this book, pages 69 to 106)

When Moses understood his special calling by God, at the Burning Bush, he received this promise for his suffering companions:

> *I have decided that I will bring them out of Egypt, where they are being treated cruelly, and will take them to a rich and fertile land.* Exodus 3:17

The promise was fulfilled at the first Passover.

> Read Exodus 12:21–28

This Passover ritual celebrates God's gracious *liberation* of Israel from slavery. The Jewish people have faithfully kept the memory of it to this day (see v.24), knowing that liberation from Egypt was only the first step in the *universal* liberation God has destined for *all the people* of the world.

Matthew saw Jesus against the backdrop of this Law, these Prophets, and this Promised Liberation. According to him, it is the community gathered around Jesus, and not pharisaic Judaism, which is the true continuation of the Old Testament.

D3 Jesus and the New Community

Matthew sees the community of Christians as the legitimate successors of the Old Testament Law, Prophets and Promise. In the Acts of the Apostles, and the letters of St Paul, we are given a number of thumbnail sketches which see this new community in much the same way as Matthew did.

1 *The Coming of the Holy Spirit*

> Read Acts 2 : 1–13

The Jewish feast of 'Pentecost' or 'Weeks' (it was celebrated a week of weeks—that is 7 × 7 days—after Passover) marked the arrival of the exodus Israelites at Mount Sinai, where they covenanted themselves to be the People of God.

The Jerusalem Christians experienced their first Pentecost, 7 weeks after Easter, as an assurance that they were the New People of God. They had an overwhelming sense of being 'set on fire' by the same godly Spirit that had inspired Jesus. They were assured that the crucified Jesus, far from being dead, was alive in their midst. The 'Holy Spirit' was, as it were, a new presence of Jesus, now embodied in the Christian community. Filled with this Holy Spirit, they boldly invited *all people* to come and join them.

The imagery of wind and fire recall Old Testament manifestations of God's power and presence, especially at Mount Sinai. (See Exodus 19 : 16–20.)

The disciples received the 'gift of tongues' ('to talk in other languages' is a bad translation). It refers to the ecstatic utterings of people made aware of God's nearness. It often happened to Old Testament prophets. The scene of an *international* crowd understanding the disciples without the aid of simultaneous translation is a reversal of the Babel story. (Genesis 11:1–9)

2 Under the inspiration of the pentecostal Spirit, the Christian community is shown in action in the pen picture drawn a little later in the same chapter.

Read Acts 2 : 40–47

No doubt this passage idealizes. There is plenty of evidence in the adjoining chapters that not '*all* the believers' (v.44) were saints. None-theless, the author agrees with Matthew that the New Community *ought*:

- to have a strong sense of being chosen and special (v.40)
- to share with others their gift of healing, as Jesus did (v.43)
- therefore to form a close fellowship of heart and mind (v.44)
- therefore to share generously with each other (v.45)
- to continue worshipping in the Temple, as Jesus did (v.46)

3   The *world-wide* scope of the New Community, already suggested in the Pentecost story of chapter 2, is further illustrated in the conversion of the Ethiopian Official and the Roman captain.

Read Acts 8 : 26–40

Even today Ethiopia lies on the fringes of world affairs: how much more so in New Testament times. The Ethiopian in this story, important though he may have been at home, was an unlikely candidate for the New Community.

The story is strongly influenced by the early Christian initiation ritual of baptism, and by the Christian conviction that the prophets had foretold Jesus, even in such unlikely texts as the one of the Suffering Servant, the slaughtered Lamb of God. Followers of Jesus must be aware of the cost.

4

Read Acts 10 : 1–48

v.1–33   The conversion of Cornelius, the Roman army captain, is an important event in the development of the Church. In this first part of the account the scene is set. Cornelius is a 'religious man'—probably he followed the Jewish religion without being fully integrated through circumcision. The early Church had a problem. Were the cultural and religious traditions of the old people of God necess-ary for the New Com-munity? Did a Gentile need first to be a circum-cised Jew before he could join the New Community by baptism? This story explains Peter's struggle to sort the problem out. The question is finally cleared up at a meeting of leaders in Jerusalem. (Acts 15 : 1–35)

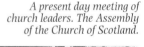

A present day meeting of church leaders. The Assembly of the Church of Scotland.

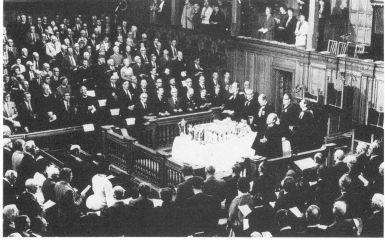

v.34–43   The Cornelius story gives occasion for an outline of the teaching of the New Community. This preached message, known as the *kerygma* (see page 2), was the earliest proclamation of faith in Jesus. Peter introduces his message with the 'breakthrough' words:

> *I now realize it is true that God treats everyone on the same basis. Whoever worships him and does what is right is acceptable to him, no matter what race he belongs to.*   (v.34–35)

The way is open, unconditionally, to outsiders—Gentiles.

v.44–48   The story concludes with an event which is a parallel to the first Pentecost. Here the Gentiles receive the Holy Spirit and are baptized into the New Community. One commentator, Nicholas Lash, points out: 'The shock the Jews received is comparable to the shock that an orthodox Christian would receive at seeing an unbaptized person admitted to the eucharist.'

5   Paul's vision of the *universal* potential of the New Community is even wider than the stories above suggest. He took the message of Jesus not only north into Asia Minor, but west into Greece, and eventually even to Italy. He had Spain and Britain in mind just before he died.

In a letter to some of his converts in Greece, he gives us a vivid picture of the New Community about the year AD50.

> Read 1 Corinthians 11:17–34

This is perhaps a surprising sketch of an early Christian Community. Paul writes with subdued anger, shocked by the cliquishness, selfishness and sheer insensitivity of his correspondents. Nonetheless his text is eloquent on many points:

- Christians met regularly to re-enact the Last Supper Jesus celebrated with his friends.
- They saw this as a ritual representation of his bloody death.
- They interpreted that death as God's new *covenant* with the world.
- They proclaimed that death as an interim expression of the *liberation* still to come (v.26).

D4 The Christian Community today

Religion can only survive on this kind of re-enactment. Each year Jews continue to re-enact their Passover ceremony. Each week Christians re-enact Jesus' Last Supper. The most fervent of them hope to pay a visit to the Holy Land. Each Spring there is a crush of Jewish pilgrims arriving to celebrate Passover 'this year in Jerusalem', and of Christian pilgrims celebrating their Easter redemption in the land of their spiritual roots. Tel Aviv airport is a maelstrom each Easter.

Christians who return to Jerusalem want to be in contact with their ancestors in faith. Is their nostalgia realistic? A recent writer explored this theme and concluded:

> Christians have, in their construction of the past, prized antiquity, stability and permanence, but the historical record shows us quite another picture... No matter how deeply we probe, how early we extend our search, we will never find an original faith. We can't go home again... There never was a home. From the beginning, Christians have been wanderers and pilgrims whose dream lies not in the past, but before them in the future.
>
> *The Myth of Christian Beginnings*   R Wilkin   Doubleday & SCM 1979

Hilaire Belloc's *Path to Rome* ends with a scene in which St Michael proudly displays before God the marvels of planet earth. God admires it, and then points down to some tiny creatures moving about. 'What are they?' 'They are the human race.' God is impressed. 'But why are some of them making such extraordinary sounds, and wearing such curious clothes?' 'They are worshipping you.' 'Oh!' says God.

If Jesus looks down from heaven at his followers, how does he react?

If Matthew was given the opportunity of returning to earth, which Christian community would he recognize as corresponding to the one he knew?

The *World Christian Encyclopedia* of 1982 states that there are 20,800 Christian denominations in the world. Are any of them—or none of them—anything like Matthew's community?

Christian pilgrims celebrating their Easter Redemption in Jerusalem

Questions and Things to Do

A   What do you know?

1   When did the Jewish nomadic tribe really become a *people*?

2   Name four prophets.

3   What did the Passover celebrate?

4   Where, in the New Testament, are the earliest descriptions of the Christian Community found?

5   What is the Festival of Weeks?

6   Outline the first Christian Pentecost. (Acts 2:1–13)

7   Why was the Ethiopian official an unlikely convert?

8   Who was Cornelius? Why is his story a turning point in the life of the early Christian Community?

9   Name two countries where Paul introduced Christianity.

10   Why was Paul angry with the community at Corinth?

B   What do you understand?

1   What passage in Matthew's Gospel is thought to be an autobiographical comment? Explain why this is so.

2   Look at the illustration on page 108. In what way does it represent Matthew's understanding of Jesus?

3   'For Matthew, there is no time of the church separated from the time of Jesus.' (Raymond Brown) Use several texts from the Gospel to discuss this comment.

4   Point out some of the imagery used in the account of the first Christian Pentecost.

5   Read the Babel story (Genesis 11:1–9). How is this reversed in the Christian Pentecost story?

C   What do you think?

1   Do you think Luke idealizes community life? (Acts 2:40–47) Give reasons for your answer.

2   Describe two 'visions' reported in Acts. Do you think the author could be describing *insights* rather than *supernatural* events? Give reasons for your answer.

3   Read Peter's speech (Acts 10:34–43) and Matthew's conclusion (Matthew 28:16–20). Assuming the author of Acts wrote later than Matthew, do you think he could have had Matthew's Gospel in front of him as he wrote Peter's speech? Give your comments.

4   What do you think makes for a good community?

D   Things to do

1   Invite people from different Christian communities to talk to you.

2   Collect photos/pictures of Christian communities and display them.

3   Create a massive collage (group activity) to illustrate your ideal community.

Useful Addresses

Irish Council of Churches 48 Elmwood Avenue, Belfast BT9 6AZ

Scottish Churches Council
Scottish Churches House, Kirk Street, Dunblane, Perthshire FK15 0AJ

Movement for a Better World (RC) Rev Adrian Smith, The Lodge, Harborne Hall, Birmingham, W. Midlands B17 0BE

Cornerstone Community 443/445 Springfield Road, Belfast BT12 7DL

The Corrymeela Community 8 Upper Crescent, Belfast BT7 1NT

Dublin Mennonite Community 4 Clonmore Villas, 92 Ballybough Road, Dublin 3

Taizé 71250 Taizé-Community, France

Useful Reading

E F Schumacher *Small is Beautiful* Abacus 1970

D5 Community Today

Christianity is a family of monotheistic faiths which in various ways find in Jesus a key to the relation of man with God. It has and will continue to have almost as much internal diversity as Hinduism ... God can be believed in and served in as many ways as there are people. Don Cupitt

Armenian Christians in the Holy Sepulchre, Jerusalem

The Salvation Army sing their message in the streets

Christian community today

Christians today number about a thousand million. Over the years believers have split into branches, distinct in their belief and worship. The three main branches that have emerged are:
- The Roman Catholic Church—mainly in the West
- The Orthodox Church—mainly in the East
- The Churches of the Protestant Reformation (Church of England, Church of Wales, Church of Scotland, Church of Ireland, Presbyterian, Baptist, Methodist, etc.)

In each denomination there are liberals, radicals, conservatives and moderates. Hence Cupitt's comment.

These *Amish Christians in Pennsylvania* show a remarkable single-mindedness in their lifestyle. They are a conservative community, persecuted over the years for refusing any alliance with the State. They live in utter simplicity, accepting no help from modern technology.

Do not store up riches for yourself here on earth.   Matthew 6:19

The churches of the *Protestant Reformation*, like the Lutheran community developed in close alliance with the State. They have flourished where their kind of Christianity has become the State religion. They emphasize the authority of the Bible.

Man cannot live on bread alone, but needs every word that God speaks.
Matthew 4:4

The *Pentecostal churches* also emphasize the Bible. They have their roots in the Black Southern States of America, where suffering and discrimination have given the people an understanding of a crucified redeemer. But they are also deeply aware of the Spirit of the living Christ in their midst. Their meetings are informal and lively usually with joyful singing.

[He] will baptize you with the Holy Spirit and fire.   Matthew 3:11

Go back to the Acts of the Apostles 2:43–47

In what way are Christian communities today like or unlike the community of Matthew's day? The way in which a community is *structured* reveals what sort of community it is. Look at these two different structures of Christian community—(both are from the Roman Catholic experience).

1   *The model of the Church bequeathed us by the Council of Trent was of a hierarchical Church.. a pyramidical structure with the Pope at its peak. At the base were the laity, the recipients of authority which always passed from top to bottom. At the Second Vatican Council (1963–65) the world's bishops rejected [this model]. There had been a change of thinking going on in the Church, from conceiving herself as a hierarchical society to seeing herself as a COMMUNITY; from a pyramid to a circle.*

Tomorrow's Parish   *Adrian Smith 1983*

A 'base community' in South America. Roman Catholic lay people meet in their homes.

2   The model (below) for a diocesan church structure was drawn up in 1988 for a Roman Catholic diocese. The outline plan is based upon the shape of the *traditional* church building, and its practice of worship.

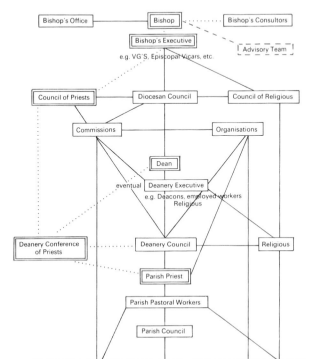

For Discussion

In groups discuss what kind of Community you think is living out the Gospel?

1 *A church congregation.*
2 *The base communities.*
3 *Christian denominations working together (ecumenism).*
4 *'Divided' peoples seeking co-operation.*
5 *Human beings understanding each other?*

An experience of communion

Sir: I would like to express publicly my sincere gratitude to the Archbishop of Canterbury and the bishops of the Anglican Communion for the warm fellowship and spontaneous friendliness extended to me and my fellow observers at the Lambeth Conference. We were made to feel at home in every possible way and given opportunities to share fully in the proceedings of the conference. Especially moving was the opportunity to participate in the daily prayer and worship which was such an important part of the conference... the hour of bible study in the morning was for... part of...

✠Cormac Murphy-O'Connor
Bishop of Arundel and Brighton
Saint Joseph's Hall
Pulborough, Sussex

...to be an ...n Conference, which ...y reported in your col...

...er to be a testimony...
is ...
affection and deep...

Base communities and the parish

The liturgy of the Mass is also enriched by meaningful involvement of the people. In Guatemala there was a Mass of solidarity with the war-scarred people of the Church of Nicaragua. During the offertory, each one placed on the altar an offering to be sent to this suffering Church. Then, according to the account, "a poor man placed on the altar a small plastic bag containing a handful of beans, nothing else. He was already returning to his place when he stopped. He looked back, then he went back. He took off his jacket, folded it carefully, affectionately, and left it on the altar together with the other offerings. . . . The temperature that evening was 10 degrees Centigrade."

In that last story we begin to see how the Christian life of the base community cannot be confined to Scripture discussion, prayer and worship, but has to spill over into social action. The new sense of social responsibility can lead to shared ventures of many kinds, from agricultural co-operatives to literacy schemes, from campaigns for sewers and clean water to sewing workshops. Often it brings an expression of communion that is truly evocative of the early Church, such as in Project Five-Two, among the metal-workers of Parque Santa Madalena in São Paulo, in which over 100 families were involved. Five families with an employed member adopted two families with no employment, and shared with them basic food items.

ALL CHILDREN TOGETHER

The All Children Together movement seeks changes in the education system of Northern Ireland that will make it possible, for parents who wish, to secure for their children an education in Shared Schools acceptable to all religious denominations and cultures, in which the Churches will provide religious education and pastoral care. Lagan College, an integrated, all-ability, post-primary college for boys and girls, opened in Belfast in September 1981. The initial 20 pupils were all fee-paying, but bursaries are available that can reduce the fees to as little as £25 per annum for low income families.

'**T**he first day or so we all pointed to our countries. The third or fourth day we were all pointing to our continents. By the fifth day we were aware of only one Earth' ■

Sultan Bin Salman al-Saud, Saudi Arabia

Which text or texts of Matthew's Gospel
would you choose to illustrate this article?
Why?

Father Dennis has transformed his church into a community centre

The Peterborough effect

Time was running out for the church of Our Lady of Lourdes, Dogsthorpe, in Peterborough when Fr Dennis Finbow arrived as the new resident priest four years ago. A run-down parish in a run-down area, it was scarcely considered viable. The huge church, one of the post-war generation built optimistically on a grand scale, complete with adjoining four-bedroom house and large garden, served a congregation of around 100 people, representing a mere five per cent of the estimated Catholic population in the surrounding council estates. It was an embarrassing waste of resources in a neighbourhood sadly lacking in amenities of any kind. A community project report revealed that the needs of young children and teenagers were not being met; there was little to offer for the many elderly housebound; there was a shortage of sport and leisure facilities; the arts and culture were non-existent.

Fr Dennis found himself seriously questioning the role of the Church in such circumstances. Inasmuch as the Church represented Christ in the world it had to be a sign of love and speak to people, he argued, it had to throw its doors open to the needs of the whole community, and not just Catholics. "I wanted people coming in," he says, "not just a granny's parlour polished for Sundays or a building locked all week while old people were imprisoned in their homes across the road."

These ideas led to the creation of a "Church and Neighbour" scheme and the foundation of the Don Bosco community centre, an ambitious project which involved giving up most of the house and a third of the church itself to make room for the two-storey building. Estimates for the job ran as high as £55,000, so with characteristic determination Fr Dennis galvanised the parish and local volunteers to do it themselves.

The work was quickly completed at an overall cost of around £20,000, money which the parish raised in record time.

The life of both parish and local community has been transformed. Today Mass attendance has grown to almost 500, while hundreds use the facilities of the centre each week for activities ranging from netball practice — the Don Bosco centre runs its own sports teams — to lunch for the handicapped. The church has become the focus of an annual arts festival attracting big names and is now the home of the Peterborough String Orchestra. The city council was so impressed it held a meeting in the church, reversed its policy of not helping churches, and provided financial support. The Manpower Services Commission has also made available some 20 people to undertake community work for the centre.

Fr Dennis is naturally delighted and hopes the venture will encourage others. "We are too apologetic in the Church", he says. "We are drifting and time is running out. But there are not so much problems, only opportunities." A local resident put it simply: "We used to walk past the church never thinking of stepping inside; but now it's like a second home."

A Final Word

THE LESSON

Then Jesus took his disciples up the mountain
and gathering them around him he taught them
saying
blessed are the poor in spirit for theirs is the kingdom of heaven
blessed are the meek
blessed are they that mourn
blessed are the merciful
blessed are they who thirst for justice
blessed are all the concerned
blessed are you when persecuted
blessed are you when you suffer
be glad and rejoice for your reward is great in heaven
try to remember what I'm telling you

Then Simon Peter said
> *will this count?*
and Andrew said
> *will we have a test on it?*
and James said
> *when do we have to know it for?*
and Philip said
> *how many words?*
and Bartholomew said
> *will I have to stand up in front of the*
> *others?*
and John said
> *the other disciples didn't have to learn this*
and Matthew said
> *how many marks do we get for it?*
and Judas said
> *what is it worth?*
and the other disciples likewise.

Then one of the Pharisees who was present
asked to see Jesus' lesson plan
and inquired of Jesus
his terminal objectives in the cognitive domain

and Jesus wept.

Don Linehan

Index